The Entrepreneur
Blueprint

How to Develop Your Darkest Storms into a Thriving Business

Carla R. Cannon

CANNONPUBLISHING

ALSO BY CARLA R. CANNON

The Power in Waiting

A Single Woman's Focus

Write the Book Already!

A Trailblazer State of Mind

A Trailblazer's Guide to SUCCESS

All available at www.CarlaCannon.com

The Entrepreneur
Blueprint

*How to Develop Your Darkest Storms into a
Thriving Business*

Carla R. Cannon

CANNONPUBLISHING

Cannon Publishing
P.O. Box 1298
Greenville, NC 27835
Office: 888-502-2228

Printed in the United States of America. First Printing, 2016

ISBN-13:978-1530965113

ISBN-10:153096511X

Quantity Sales. Special discounts are available on quantity purchases by corporations, associations, and others. For details, contact Carla Cannon at Carla@WomenOfStandard.org or www.CarlaCannon.com.

Dedication

• •

To every person who has a dream of firing their boss and hiring themselves as COO this book is for you! Dreams are real but only if you are willing to do the work, face your fears and step out of the norm. Get ready to embrace your new normal! I am here to remind you that anything is possible with hard work, dedication, commitment, fervency, and resilience!

- Carla

Contents

INTRODUCTION 1
Why This Book is For YOU

CHAPTER ONE..12
How it All Began/My Journey

CHAPTER TWO...27
Identifying Your Passion

CHAPTER THREE 41
Developing Your Gift into a Thriving Business

CHAPTER FOUR 55
Mistakes Aspiring Entrepreneurs Make

CHAPTER FIVE 125
The Danger of Chasing More Than One Rabbit

CHAPTER SIX..137
Characteristics of a Kingdom Entrepreneur

CHAPTER SEVEN 147
Pearls of Wisdom for Entrepreneurs

CHAPTER EIGHT 155
How to Build Your Business While Working a 9 to 5

CHAPTER NINE 167
Fire Your Boss & Hire Yourself as COO

About the Author 185

Introduction
Why This Book is For YOU

If you have picked up this book, *The Entrepreneur Blueprint: How to Develop Your Darkest Storms into a Thriving Business* I am certain you are interested in learning how you can take some of the most painful experiences in your life and turn them around to work in your favor. This is something I am honestly still learning how to master myself and have honestly yet gotten a full grip on it. I too had often heard that my pain had purpose, but I could never seem to accept that as my reality.

Now I am a Kingdom girl therefore I am aware of the scripture that tells us all things will work together for our good but come on now. How often have you read scriptures that you yourself didn't believe or couldn't seem to grab the concept of? Right. Exactly!

I couldn't accept the fact all the hell I'd been through would eventually work out for my good one day. The abuse, being the black sheep of my family, having labels placed on me, struggling in my identity…. No…you can't be serious about all those things eventually coming together to work for my good?

But now after experiencing a greater level of spiritual maturity and going deeper in my faith I can tell you that it will all work together for your good despite how you may feel currently. I understand how hard it is to see how some of the most devastating moments of your life will actually work out for your good. Trust me I have been there but when you decide to snatch back your power and own your truth success and deliverance for your life is inevitable!

The mere fact that you have picked up this book is apparent to me that you are finally ready to embrace what I call, a *new normal.* Not sure what that is? Well, in the words of one of my favorite comedians, Kevin Hart, let me explain (ha!).

According to how many of us were raised, we were taught to graduate from high school, attend college not so we could learn how to lead others and run our own businesses but so we could get what our parent's called a J-O-B.

Many of us were then encouraged to get married, have a few kids and then uhhh... die. Pretty much that's the current normal. I believe I saw on social media one time where someone said, *"I was created to do more than just pay bills and die!"*

I agree with this statement wholeheartedly and it is past time for you to also understand that as a woman you were created to do more than just lay on your back and push out babies. As a man you were created to do more than take out the trash and do push-ups in the gym to show that you are a *real man.*

Life is about so much more than many of us fail to realize. One of the greatest books I've ever read outside of The Holy Bible was, *The Purpose Driven Life* by Rick Warren. What he talks about in his book is how one can uncover their hidden potential and tap into their inner gifts in essence of finding out what on earth they were created for.

As an aspiring or current Kingdom Entrepreneur it is important that you incorporate prayer and fasting as you seek the Lord for wisdom in regard to which business venture you should launch first. As it relates to me you will learn that I began my journey not really knowing this is where I would end up. I loved journaling but it still shocked me, and many others, when I wrote my first book-- as well as it becoming a best seller!

Well, then again, my mom and my aunts say they were not surprised when I wrote my first book because I was always writing as a young girl. I used to buy tons of journals and keep them because (1) they were so pretty and (2) I couldn't wait to fill them all up with my thoughts, prayers, and ideas. Trust me, there were a lot of them!

One of the things I've learned along this journey called life is that all things truly work together for our good. Although it may not feel like it at the moment, but it is indeed working for your good. Every job I've had has helped me operate in the current field I am in. Naturally I had great administrative skills but lacked people skills.

My inability to function properly with others stemmed from me being diagnosed (as a child) as being behaviorally emotionally handicapped and basically what they were saying was I was incapable of getting along with others. This disorder basically meant that I was incapable of managing my emotions and they truly did often get the best of me. But we will get into this later when I share my story with you.

As you journey through life you will be in pursuit of two things:

(a) What is your life purpose?

(b) What is your vision?

Let's talk about that for a moment.

Purpose VS Vision: Creating Vision Boards

I like to identify our purpose as our WHY and WHAT with your vision being your HOW. Why we were created and what we were created to do during our short time on this earth. In the book *The Purpose Driven Life* (I mentioned previously) Warren does an exceptional job breaking it down into 40 chapters that takes his readers on a very strategic journey to identifying their life purpose.

Believe it or not, all that you have experienced whether good or bad from the day you were born to this current day were all a part of your divine purpose. There are no wasted experiences except for the ones you refuse to grow from and overcome so you can share with others how you made it out of what once had you bound and how they can too!

Now, in addition to purpose, we also need to have vision. Vision is our HOW. How we plan to walk out our purpose in our daily lives. One concept that many visionaries are grasping and promoting is the importance of creating a vision board.

In case you are not aware, a vision board is where you cut out photos, graphics and words of things, people, and places (out of a magazine or you can print them off online) that you desire to do, meet and go in your lifetime. Then you place them (using tape or glue) on a board and the key is to keep it in a place that is visible to use as motivation each day you wake up to remind you of what your focus should be.

The problem with vision boards is people tend to stop there. In a previous Vision Casting Mastermind Group, I shared with my clients that the first steps to creating a vision board is to first identify what you desire to do in and with your life.

In doing so, I recommended them to create a list of 20 things they wanted to do in life. I typically prefer them to list 100 things they desire to do in their lifetime and not to overthink it but as things come to their mind to list them. They can include things such as:

■ Lose 20 pounds

■ Get married

■ Meet Oprah

- Appear as a guest on The Dr. Phil Show

- Launch a business

- Write a book

- Give birth to a child

- Receive your doctorate

- Travel to Europe

You get the point, right? Well, after they create the list, I encourage them to then create a vision board with one side being a visual of their overall life and the other side focused on the upcoming year they are preparing to enter.

So, for example, if you were creating a vision board you would place on one side pictures, places and things that resemble your overall future. It would be a mixture of all or many of the things I mentioned in the list above.

However, for the specific year you are preparing to enter you will cut out only pictures and words that reflect all you desire to do specifically in that year alone. Vision boards are typically created at the end of the year to prepare you for the upcoming year and help you become laser focused on assignments and tasks you hope to accomplish.

So, at this time you have a double-sided vision board; one side is a visual of your overall life and the other side are strategic goals you have for the upcoming year.

Now, here's where so many people drop the ball which prevents them from transitioning from goal setters to goal achievers:

"A goal without a strategic plan of action is simply a wish!"

After you create this double-sided vision board you must NOT stop there. Next, grab a pen and pad and list your goals one by one and then develop a strategic plan of action next to each of them stating

HOW you plan to make this dream a reality. Remember your HOW is the vision and your WHAT and WHY is your purpose.

For example, if you desire to receive your PH. D here are the proper steps you may have to take:

1. Apply for college

2. Apply for financial aid

3. Complete bachelor's program

4. Complete master's program

5. Receive PH. D

6. *BONUS: Stay focused amid all of it.

As you can see there is a *process* to positioning yourself to be able to dream with your eyes wide open! Once you do this for each item you have placed on your list (starting with the side of your vision board that is for the upcoming year) this helps you become laser focused on what matters, eliminate what doesn't and builds momentum for the more you see it, the more excited you'll become!

The word, *process* could also be applied as it relates to *The Entrepreneur Blueprint,* and I will be sharing more with you in chapters to come. I always encourage my readers and everyone I encounter to never despise small beginnings. But to always remember we must each crawl before we walk.

What do I mean by that? Although you may currently be punching a clock every day, making someone else rich, the fact is if you have an exit plan you can make your life so much more enjoyable if you understand that your J-O-B helps FUND your business.

So many people want to just up and quit their jobs however, I believe that in all we do we must develop a strategic plan of action to implement and use as a guide (or blueprint) for our success.

"He who fails to plan, plans to fail..."- Winston Churchill

Within the pages of this book, I will be sharing with you how to enjoy your current job knowing that where you are is not where you will always be. However, you must also keep in mind that you can't exit and transition into your next place or assignment in destiny until you complete the work that is currently presented before you.

Before you can accept a new assignment provided by our Creator, you must first ace the tests that are presented before you today. One of the things I learned at the last job I worked (before taking the courageous step into full time entrepreneurship) was that in life we can only take it one day at a time.

Sure, I have big dreams, however, I can't focus so much on my dreams that I fail to enjoy the moment I am blessed with now. I had to learn to embrace my current job even when I knew I had a greater call and deeper sense of purpose. But it wasn't until I changed my mindset and thought process regarding my job that I was able to submit my two-week resignation and enter into full time entrepreneurship.

Previously I hosted a workshop entitled, *How to Build Your Business WHILE Working a 9 to 5* where I shared how I built my business over the course of four years while working in corporate America. My goal is to help you get rid of this false sense of hope that you can't be happy until you are doing what you love full time. You can be happy NOW!

The key to coming off your job is having the ability to replace the income your J-O-B brought in, on a consistent basis or residually. I share a step-by-step guide on how to do this via my self-study coaching program entitled, *Fire Your Boss.* (Learn more at www.CarlaCannon.com.)

Within the pages of this book, I will also be sharing exactly what I did step by step while working my 9 to 5 that positioned me to put in my two-week notice and never look back.

Chapter 1
How It All Began/My Journey

I always knew I was different growing up. I didn't fit in with the other kids and I always wanted to be like the one person I thought was the most popular and talented girl I knew: my sister.

You see, my sister was no ordinary girl, she could sing, rap, dance her behind off, play double-dutch like no other, was a beast on the basketball court and on top of that everyone seemed to just love her. I recall my sister making good grades and not really giving my mom any trouble.

Then I was born. I was considered my mother's *problem child*. I was the one that gave her a "run for her money" as the older generation would say. I remember being a skinny little girl with long black ponytails and the cutest smile ever with only one deep dimple in my *left* cheek.

I can recall starting off very happy as a child, for I had my mom and my dad in my life. I was always told I looked just like him; he has a very deep dimple in his *right* cheek (well he has two dimples but the right one is the deepest- HA!).

My sister and I grew up and although we had the same mom, we had different dads and my mom was married to my dad who was in the military and that is how I ended up being born in Heidelberg, Germany.

To make a long story short, my mom and dad decided to split, and we moved back to the states when I was about two years old. I remember always wanting to be just like my sister. But I was labeled as ADHD (attention deficit hyperactivity disorder-refers to an individual who is hyperactive and can't control their impulses). I was also identified as being Behaviorally Emotionally Handicapped which is a disability that impacts a person's ability to effectively recognize, interpret, control and express fundamental emotions.

Because of these two diagnoses I had trouble making friends and maintaining relationships because my condition (or label they placed on me) was never really explained to me but instead I was placed on Ritalin which was a medication that was to keep me pretty much calm, cool, collected and out of the grown folks' way.

I was extremely talkative as a child. I was very similar to Kevin from the movie, Home Alone. I am sure you remember him. Kevin was always talking and into something, but he was an extremely bright kid, however, he was different. Because he was different, he was often identified as being weird or a troublemaker. But truth is Kevin just wanted to be loved and accepted like everyone else. But what happened? Like many of our troubled teens today, Kevin had no one to take up time with him.

His parents were always busy, and his brother, Bud wasn't the nicest and had the weirdest looking girlfriend but had the nerve to talk about Kevin. Because again he was *different.*

That was me; different. I remember being prescribed and placed on Ritalin by my therapist to help me focus because I was always fidgeting and moving in my seat and talking out of turn. I was basically getting on my teachers' nerves to the point many of them grew tired of dealing with me.

But instead of helping me, this medication began to make me itchy, and it controlled my appetite to the point that I wouldn't want anything to eat. I'm sure by now you have a visual and can imagine that I was nothing but skin and bones through most of my childhood. Yep, that was me.

I remember literally sitting on one spot on the sofa for hours while my cousins would be in the other room playing, or my family would be playing cards. I'd be glued to the seat in the living room, quiet and out of everyone's way to the point I felt totally invisible at times.

This medication that was supposed to *help* me was literally hurting and driving me crazy. Not only did it make me itch, but it also made me talk to myself often. I believe this is why I enjoyed playing with Barbie dolls so much because it made me feel as if I had people around me, but it was only me, Ken, Barbie and the others whom I created different names and voices for.

To only make matters worse, due to my defiant behavior in school I was placed in a Special Education class with other students who had severe learning disabilities.

Now, I was an extremely smart kid however, because of my behavior I was placed in this class with other students who could barely read and struggled to do simple subtraction and addition problems.

I remember having to walk in a single file line (in middle school) to go to lunch while all the other students would laugh and make faces at me. I was stuck in this class with other students who physically had things wrong with them, and then here I was this beautiful big eyed, long hair and nothing, but skin and bones little girl and I remember the onset feelings of depression even as a child.

My elementary and middle school years were pretty rough however; I managed to get through them. I grew to the point that I would pretend to take my medicine but would put it under my tongue and spit it out after I left the water fountain.

But shortly after they could tell I didn't take it because I'd be talking up something and it was as if I really couldn't control myself. I later learned that the reason why I talked so much at school was because my voice was literally stripped from me in my home.

I remember being asked publicly by several of my teachers, *"Carla, did you take your medicine?"* I remember being so embarrassed about it and that would cause me to act out even more. To make matters worse I could recall family members laughing and telling my mom, *"She need a pill,"* whenever I acted out.

Funny thing about it all is although this was years ago tears still fill my eyes because no one ever stopped to ask me how I felt or why I was always acting out at school. It was as if I didn't matter, that no one could see me. I felt invisible. So, I acted out to be heard which was actually my cry for help. Sadly, no one could hear me.

Privately back at home I was witnessing my mother and her then husband fighting and arguing regularly. He would also physically abuse me as well. I remember having to hold a pitcher of salt for hours at a time while being threatened not to allow my arms to fall or I'd get hit with the belt.

Now, so you have a clear picture I would have to stand straight with my hands out forward (in front of me) with my hands cupped, holding the big blue and white pitcher of salt and that would be my punishment for that day. Do you know that to this day I never buy the big thing of salt for this very reason? I only buy the small saltshakers and once they are gone, I go out and buy another one. It's amazing how some things can stick with us even through our adulthood.

I can remember some family members thinking this form of punishment was so funny that while tears were streaming down my face, they took pictures of me while I was holding the salt which again was a form of punishment granted to me by my stepfather. I can remember seeing the photographs and even laughing later with family members who thought it was so funny, when I was really crying inside and totally embarrassed.

Another form of punishment was what my stepdad called *bobbing*. Now to picture this, imagine squatting down to pick something up but you remain in that position. You come up and down, up, and down. Your legs are remaining in a squat or bob position, and you slightly lift up and down for hours (close to the floor.)

When, I say hours, I do mean just that. I can remember one time having to sit next to the table as my mom, her husband and their friends played cards and as usual I did something and got in trouble for it. I think it was the time I spilled fingernail polish on the floor and tried to hide it, but I honestly can't remember. It was something. Well, as punishment I had to *bob* the entire time they played cards.

Now if your family is anywhere like mine, they could play cards all night! I don't want to exaggerate my story, but I know I was *bobbing* for at least three hours at the table while they played cards. Again, I felt ignored and as if I didn't matter and every now and then my stepfather would look at me only to ensure I was still moving and did not lose my balance.

But no one would say anything because they grew used to being around the hyperactive little girl who talked a lot and stayed in trouble. This was our *normal* and our neighbors who came over to play cards were like family and they were used to it as well. Therefore, no one said a word. The rule was if you ever stop *bobbing* or lose your balance you would get a slap on the back (not behind) with the belt. I will never forget the pain I would feel in my legs after being released to go to my room. I could barely walk or even feel my legs.

Another punishment would be to come home, do my chores, take a bath, and go straight to bed. This would include weekends also. I remember feeling so alone. Sadly, my sister and I were never close and perhaps it was because we were four years a part. I always felt like her nagging little sister. Now, she would never let anyone bother me, but we didn't have a close bond as sisters; not like the one I have always desired and dreamed of. However, I did grow close with my stepsister.

My sister and I used to love when, let's call her Deborah, would come over because her dad would be the nicest ever and we would do fun stuff the entire weekend she was there. Believe it or not during this time there was no arguing, no fighting and I barely got in trouble for anything. Ironic huh? Right.

We absolutely loved it when Deborah was around, because her dad would turn into the nicest man in the world. But boy when she would leave it's like he would flip a switch and it would be like Nightmare on Elm Street.

Funny thing is it wasn't until I was in my 20's that I learned Deborah's dad had *never* spanked her once in her life. Now, Deborah and I were four years a part just like my older sister and I were four years a part. You would have thought her, and I were biological sisters; we were just that close.

Fast forward a bit: I remember the day her and I relationship changed forever when I was about 24 years old (I believe it was) and one day I am not sure how the conversation came up, but I finally shared with her all of the bad stuff her dad did to my mom and I.

I went on to share with her how he used to beat me (those surely were NOT spankings) and I was wild and would run around the room to keep from getting hit and he would sit on my head and beat me until my nose would bleed.

Sad thing is I witnessed my mom standing right there allowing this man to do this to me while saying, *"Don't beat her while you are mad!"* But my mom too was afraid of him and there was sadly nothing she could do at this time. Or so she felt.

I remember Deborah crying like a baby and it was extremely hard for her to accept because the man who literally was my worst nightmare she viewed as *The World's Greatest Dad.* Sadly, our sacred sisterhood ended a few years after that when I decided to share my story through my first book, *The Power in Waiting.* Within the pages of that book, I shared my story of the abuse I experienced with her dad and how it affected me not only as a child but as a young woman which flowed over into my adulthood. I remember receiving the most painful email from her ever after she purchased my book.

She pretty much told me I was playing the victim and used quite a few choice words that I honestly can't remember but I do recall the tears that streamed down my face as I read the letter from the girl who I had known literally all my life. I When I first met her, she was four and I was eight (if I'm not mistaken) or perhaps even a little younger, she may have been two. I'm not good with remembering those details.

Deborah and I had a lot of history together therefore, it was extremely hard to let her go. We used to play with our Barbie dolls together, we sung "Baby, Baby, Baby" by TLC together at an amusement park (I still have the VHS somewhere); she and I were extremely close and even remained close through our early twenties. Even with the distance. I remember witnessing her win homecoming queen (or some type of award for her school during a game.) I was present when she received her bachelor's degree in accounting. I was also in her life when she purchased her first home. She was in my daughter and I life and she would always travel home to attend Patience (my daughter)'s birthday parties.

Our separation was truly bittersweet but nevertheless in life you have to learn to love people enough to let them go. I recently heard Deborah is getting married. I am extremely happy for her yet sad at the same time because we vowed that whoever got married first, we would be each other's maid of honor. I guess that'll never happen. Tears......

Back to My Childhood

I always felt very alone, isolated, and unwanted as a child. Due to my defiance, I remember overhearing one of my aunties tell my mom to send me away. But my mom refused. It's funny how even today as a grown woman I can remember so many vivid details of my childhood. It still brings tears to my eyes because it took me years to overcome and some things, I am still breaking off of my life even with being in my 30's. Childhood programming is no joke but well worth enduring the process in order to experience true freedom.

I remember my mom and stepdad always fighting over money and I would be in my bed scared to death. My sister would be across the hall in her room, and I remember us both being two scared girls stuck, hearing our mother screaming and all the fighting. But, after a while it became our normal. Not that we became used to it or comfortable, but it was a part of our daily life and routine. We would get up in the morning, eat breakfast, go to school, come home, complete our homework and chores, watch a little TV, get to bed and then we would become awakened by the yelling, screaming, and fighting. My mom worked nights and my stepfather worked days so most of their arguments took place at night which caused me to flinch a lot in my sleep (I still do this to this day).

One day my entire life changed and shifted forever. One night my mom and my stepdad had got into another fight, and I guess this time my sister was sick of it. My sister was getting older, and I believe she was playing basketball and was getting a few muscles (ha!) Again, please be patient with me because the strange thing is I can remember specific events of my childhood, but I can't remember the exact age I was when certain incidents occurred. But I remember specific details to a "t."

I remember being interviewed on The Jewel Tankard Show and she asked me what age I was when the physical abuse began with my stepdad and out of nervousness, I said 11 but later after speaking to my mom I learned I was actually 6. I am never good at matching my age with the events, but I can still remember all of the horrible things that happened to me during my childhood. Honestly, if I could forget it all I would! Take it away Jesus!!!!!!!

Back to the story: that night my stepdad had hit my mom and this time my sister jumped in it, and I remember hearing her tell him, *"This is the last time you gonna hit my mama!"* I remember witnessing him pick my sister up and throwing her either on the couch or their bed. All I recall is him having my sister up in the air and she was literally punching him in the face repeatedly.

That night, my sister went to bed with a huge knife under her pillow and I recall my mom saying that *something* (we now have identified as Holy Spirit) told her to go and look under my sister's pillow. She did and that is when she found the knife. When she approached my sister asking why she had it I remember hearing my sister say, *"Because if he hit you again, I am going to kill him!"*

I remember seeing the look on my sister's face, she was so serious, and I want to say tears were streaming down her face. Now, this would have been a great moment for my mom to hug my sister and tell her everything was going to be okay. But the truth is, my mom wasn't a hugger. Neither is my sister; however, my daughter and I are very loving and affectionate individuals. My mom often showed her love growing up by what she did for us. But I don't recall hearing the words, "I love you" that often unless I was saying it to my mom first.

Now, by no means am I trying to make my mom look bad for she is a great mother, and I don't blame her for any decisions she has made. She did what she felt was the best with the knowledge and wisdom she had at that time. We have talked about this on several occasions however, to this day I still don't think my mother or even my sister know the effect these things had on me as a child.

I honestly believe this is the reason I'm not married, and my daughter is a teenager. I didn't want a man in my home that was not her father because I saw how my stepdad treated his daughter versus how he treated my sister and I (as well as my mother.) Therefore, to this day it has always only been my daughter and I in our home (her father is very active in her life but resides outside of our home). I didn't want the same things to happen to her that happened to me. I felt I had to protect my daughter and I did so by dating outside the home.

After the knife incident, instead of my mom packing us up and saying this is it, enough is enough. She transitioned my sister out of the home and sent her to go and live with her dad. I remember that being the worst day of my life because now I was forced to have to be at home with 'Freddy Krueger' all by myself because my mom worked nights.

Can you just imagine how horrible I felt? More importantly to this day I always wondered how my sister felt being that my mom kept me with her but made her go live with her dad. This is not something my mom or my sister talks about. Ask me, I think we all need therapy but hey…I'm just saying.

Fast Forward

Now that you pretty much have a clear picture in regard to my childhood let's take it a step further because it does get worst. At 14 years old I lost my virginity to a guy who all I knew was his first and last name. I also thought he really liked me but later found out that he didn't. He was only after one thing. You know that *thing* Lauryn Hill talks about in her song, *"Doo Wop: That Thing."* Yeah, that was him.

After opening Pandora's Box, I became sexually promiscuous combined with drinking and smoking marijuana. I became pregnant with my daughter at 17 years old during my senior year in high school. I then gave birth to my daughter at 18 years old and here I was responsible for this beautiful life when my life itself was spiraling out of control.

Due to never dealing with my past, my biological father who wrestled with alcohol addiction and was in and out of my life, I was completely over men and had lost all attraction to them. I found myself liking women (one woman at first) which later led to me engaging in the homosexual lifestyle for over five years of my life.

Even now as I think back on all the things that could have happened to me, I am truly grateful that God spared me. I remember hanging out with people I didn't know and spoking marijuana with them and having sex with people I had only known for a short period of time.

I remember being close friends with people who were using cocaine and to this day I bless God for not allowing that to be a part of my story because who is to say how I would have ended up had I gotten caught up in heavy drugs and alcohol. Now, there was a season of my life where I had to have Hennessy to go to bed every night for about thirty days. I remember the pain being so great in my life that like my dad, I tried to drink it away.

By the grace of God, I ended up kicking that habit out of fear of being like my dad, who currently still battles alcohol addiction in his 50's (please keep him in your prayers).

By this point in my life, I found myself trying to go to college for Medical Assisting, but it would never work because I did not have a passion for it. Although I always landed great jobs in the medical field (without a degree) I was still always in pursuit of something more; greater.

Although I always had a great job, I couldn't keep any money because I spent more than I made and was horrible at budgeting. I often found myself having to call my mom to bail me out by helping me with bills. She would run to my rescue every time which honestly became my crutch that I used right before entering my 30's.

I remember not feeling as if I had any natural gifts like my sister. Remember, she could sing, dance, jump double-dutch like no other, she was good at math, popular and everyone loved her. In my eyes she was normal and as a child I heard, *"Why can't you be like..."* For the sake of this book, let's call her Tina.

I would always hear, *"Why can't you be more like Tina?!"* I felt like my sister was normal and I was the weirdo. I would often cry myself to sleep wishing I too were normal, loved and even liked. Little did I know I was created in *His* image and had a lot to offer the world than what I had yet to tap into.

But one day my life changed forever. Now, my sister and I grew up in the church. My mother's side of the family were Christian, but my father's side were Jehovah's Witnesses. So, I would go to church on Sunday as a child, but I'd also attend the Kingdom Hall with my paternal grandmother, Rachel whom I miss dearly. She died in a car accident when I was around twelve years old and that too was a tragic moment in my life-- To lose my grandmother whom I loved dearly. I remember receiving the phone call that she had died, and I literally had no reaction.

I just went right back to doing what I was doing. It didn't set in until the funeral that I had literally lost the only biological grandmother I had ever known.

I never knew my maternal grandmother; I didn't remember her rather because I was about two or three years old when she died of an aneurysm.

So here I was a mother, confused in life, had no clue what my purpose was, dating women, and engaging in activities that went directly against my beliefs as a Christian. I remember in the midst of all of my transitions I would cry out to God and asked Him to help me. This was the night I could literally remember feeling God wrap me in His arms as I wept quietly and cried myself to sleep.

I slowly began to take steps back toward Christ by attending a local church. I remember the pastor had mentioned the church going on a 40 day fast while reading, *The Purpose Driven Life* by Rick Warren which was also 40 chapters. Our assignment was to fast eating fruits and vegetables only while reading one chapter per day. I must admit completing this 40-day book transformed my life.

During this time, I began to journal a lot and it began to become clear to me that I enjoyed writing and encouraging others. While I continued to nurture my relationship with Christ, I began to study His word and do my best to apply it to my life and do exactly what it said.

I found it to be a struggle but sooner than later I finally developed a system that worked for my daughter and me. I was learning more about the blood of Jesus and how to properly conduct spiritual warfare and declare war against him. I remember one day asking God to take my life and do what He may. This was the day I came to the end of Carla and Christ literally rose in me.

Sure, it took time to overcome my dark past and honestly there are still some things I battle with even today. But what keeps me going is being reminded that I am not my issue, and I am chosen by Christ. Just as King David has trials and issues in the Bible, he was still identified as a man after God's own heart.

Anyone close to me knows that David is my favorite person from the Bible. Because He was jacked up and I feel I can relate so much with his story. David was the least of his brothers to be chosen. But it was him that was appointed to be king and defeat the Philistine named, Goliath.

I also feel my story relates to that of Joseph who went from the pit to the palace after being sold into slavery by his own siblings. Unfortunately, we all have things we have dealt with and are still working to overcome but my friend I am here to tell you that it is possible to develop your darkest storms into a thriving business.

In March 2013 I decided to pen my pain and share my story with the world. My first book (of many) was entitled, *The Power in Waiting: What Do You Do When What God Said, Doesn't Line Up with What You See?* In sharing my story God used me to help set a lot of women (and men) free from their past. Many began to rise unashamed of their past and determined to learn how to make all that happened *to* them work *for* them. Little did I know this was the first of *many* books I'd write. The rest is history after that.

Chapter 2
Identifying Your Passion
PAIN+ PASSION = PURPOSE

After all I had endured in life: labels being placed on me as a child, rejection, being told I'd never amount to anything, teenage pregnancy, sexual promiscuity, abortions, homosexuality I had no clue how God was going to use all of my pain to take me on a never-ending journey of fulfilling my life purpose.

Remember I shared earlier that our purpose is WHY and WHAT. Why we were created and what we were created to do. After I began to attend church more frequently, I began to dive deeper into God's word which led to me writing more and more in my journal. By this time, I was looking forward to writing each day and sharing my thoughts and prayers to God.

I remember one day while I was trying to break free from a homosexual relationship I was in, with my then girlfriend, I heard the Lord say, *"You are a Woman of Standard."* I remember crying like a baby because it was as if I literally heard God's audible voice. What I didn't realize was happening in that very moment was that I was giving birth to what would be not only my ministry but a global movement for women.

That's when Women of Standard was born. My heart at this time was to love others through their hurt and help them overcome hurt, pain and betrayal like I too had experienced. I began to randomly select people I felt led to encourage each week and I would personally type up letters and mail it to them personally.

I know I could have emailed it, but I wanted to go a step further in making each woman feel special. I wanted her to know that she was loved, thought about and be reminded that she could make it through any storm life presented before her because we were created to soar!

After doing that for some time, I later transitioned into developing my writings into a newsletter. I remember consistently releasing the newsletters over the course of 12 months and by this time I learned that I really enjoyed writing. It would be the first thing I would think of in the morning and the last thing I thought of when I went to bed at night.

In addition to releasing a monthly newsletter entitled, Women of Standard, I also began to blog, and this is how the writer within was unleashed. I found great joy and release being in front of my laptop writing out powerful messages to inspire and empower others. I began to develop a following on social media because not only did I print out the newsletters and mail them out to individuals in the community, but I also shared the full newsletter on social media outlets such as Facebook.

After receiving such great feedback from the recipients, a male friend of mine at that time encouraged me to develop the newsletter into a magazine. Mind you I had a medical background and had a degree in NOTHING, and I sure didn't know where to begin with a magazine.

However, he agreed to design it for me free of charge and we transitioned Women of Standard from a newsletter to a magazine. I remember by my fourth month; I had landed my very first "celebrity" interview with Dr. Jamal Bryant (for our Men of

Standard column within the magazine). I remember only having 15 minutes and I was nervous as all get out, but I got through it.

I went on to grow and expand Women of Standard Magazine across the globe for the next two years and everything was going great until the team I had begun to crumble. By this time, I had over 20 contributors, an editor and leadership team in which we conducted monthly team calls, etc.

Mind you I was running a global magazine *while* working my 9 to 5. I would work 9 to 5 but would rise early to check my emails and reply to individuals we had reached out to regarding interviews. I would schedule interviews during my lunch breaks at work.

While my coworkers were sitting in the lounge room gossiping or talking about nothing, I was in my car interviewing people such as Stellar Award Winner, Kierra Sheard, Gospel Artist Lisa Page Brooks, Best Selling Author and Speaker Valorie Burton and the highlight of my career as a publisher was interviewing legendary, Yolanda Adams!!!

I will never forget these moments for I enjoyed every part of it, and I learned a lot in the process. I shared this story so I could point out a few quick points I learned during the two years I operated as the Founder of Women of Standard Magazine:

1. **Always keep it simple.**
   The less people you have in your personal space, the better. The more people the greater the drama and conflicting opinions and perspectives.

2. **Be careful who you allow into your inner circle.**
   Whoever has your ear, has your heart. Guard it with ALL diligence.

3. **Develop a Solid Prayer Life**
   Receive complete instructions in prayer from God then obey.

4. **Be careful who you allow on your team**
   Everyone will not respect your platform, therefore, be careful who you invite on it.

5. **Never allow anyone to talk you out of having a great mentor**
   I remember I allowed someone who was very well respected in the industry to give me bad advice which was not to allow anyone in the industry to mentor me who had not been in the business longer than five years because they would end up jealous of me. During the time I received this information I had begun mentorship with this woman who was slam across the states but because of who this woman (the person giving the advice) was who had worked with people like Bishop T.D. Jakes I took her advice and cancelled my mentoring sessions with this woman who was NOT charging me a dime to share valuable information. Because of this I ended up missing out on nurturing an extremely beneficial relationship and had I kept that connection perhaps when I ran into a deep rut with my team, she could have helped coach me out of that dilemma. But because I chose to lend the WRONG person my ear I suffered tremendously because after only two years my career as a magazine publisher ended due to not knowing how to properly handle certain issues I faced with my team. It all worked out in my favor later because I learned the magazine was a launching pad for my career and now, I can focus on Women of Standard the movement and not limit it to the magazine only.

Although the magazine ended after being in publication for only two years, I still learned a lot and by now I learned that my one of my gifts stemmed from my passion which was journaling. Being that my pen and pad became my best friends I began to develop a passion for sharing my story.

Being the Chief Editor of Women of Standard Magazine I also wrote monthly in a column entitled, Publisher's Voice. I shared marketable messages and included strategic steps on how the reader could overcome or develop a solution for a particular problem.

After releasing the magazine my passion for writing grew more intense. I began to work on my first book (or what I thought would be my first book), *Breaking Free: What to Do When You Find Yourself in an Identity Crisis.* No one could have told me this wasn't going to be my first book. It took me months to write and on the day, I completed the last chapter I heard the spirit of the Lord say, (now, don't be alarmed I believe in being spiritual *not* spooky), "Chunk it!"

I remember thinking I was literally losing it that day because I could hear the Lord clearly tell me to get rid of it. As I began to enter prayer to ensure I was discerning correctly I remember hearing in my spirit, *"If you release this book the exact way it is written right now you are going to hurt a whole lot of people."*

In addition to hearing that, I also heard the word, "Chunk it" once again. Well, by this time I was a little more mature in my Christian journey and I knew that obedience was better than sacrifice. Therefore, I immediately opened the file on my laptop and clicked delete. To take it a step further (in case I was tempted) I also went into my recycle bin and deleted it.

So, what do I do now? I thought. During this time, I remember Holy Spirit sharing with me how that book was a therapy writing process for me. It was a way for me to get out my hurt, pain, anger, frustration, and every other emotion I felt without being judged. If I felt it, I typed it and once I was done wisdom kicked in and said, "Don't you dare publish *that!*"

Key Tips to Keep in Mind While Writing a Book:

1. **Stick with sharing your own story.**

   I could not tell my mother's story therefore, certain things that happened in my life I don't discuss publicly because it would lead into telling her story. She must tell her own.

2. **Never write while wounded.**

   If you are hurt stay away from social media and do not create new products. It is only through a healed (or process of becoming healed vessel) that you will produce some of your best work.

3. **Tell the truth.**

   I remember being reached out to by a major network and after answering a series of questions (interview lasted for 30 minutes) I began to feel as if the lady wanted me to overdramatize my story. I refused to say things happened to me that didn't happen. She couldn't seem to get her mind around the fact that I was not raped or molested and ended up in homosexual relationships. Never allow anyone to pressure you into curving your story. Stick to the script and tell the truth! Never do anything for five minutes of fame. A few months later I met Jewel Tankard (wife of legendary, Ben Tankard from the hit show, Thicker Than Water) and was invited to Detroit to share my story on her show!

Back to the book: When I opened a new document Holy Spirit taught me a 7-day writing process that I now teach individuals across the globe. I took a break from writing and when I came back, I sat down for seven days straight, (no more than two hours max per sitting) and I wrote my first book (which was a memoir) entitled, *The Power in Waiting: What Do You Do When What God Said Doesn't Line Up With What You See?*

Within 24 hours my first book made the Amazon's Best Seller List and within 30 days I was awarded as a National Best-

Selling Author for Black Christian Authors! I remember sitting back saying, WOW! I did it! I actually wrote my first book.

A Moment of Reflection

Do you remember how earlier I mentioned growing up I used to want to be just like my older sister, Tina (we are calling her Tina for the sake of this book.) Well, what I didn't know was the reason I talked so much as a child was because I was born to be a speaker. The reason I enjoyed journaling so much was because I am a writer. I also learned that although I was identified as being bossy, I was a leader who simply needed direction and guidance.

Although even to this day I still admire my sister, I have learned to love myself and although I don't have natural gifts that are visible like others, I have the gifts God chose to give me. One of the things He gave me was a creative mind and an ability to think and dream BIG! That alone outweighs anything I could have ever prayed and asked God for.

Passion & Purpose

As you can see from all I have mentioned thus far it is your passion that will lead you into your purpose. It was because of the abuse, neglect, and rejection I experienced as a child that I developed a heart for hurting people who were also different (not weird, but unique). I didn't think or operate like others, I didn't fit in with the crowd, who were in situations they didn't know how to get out of. Those were the people I began to become *passionate about.*

WHAT is it that you are passionate about? List the top 5 things or areas you are passionate about.

1.

2.

3.

4.

5.

WHY are you passionate about the things you listed above? List 1 reason for each item you listed above.

1.

2.

3.

4.

5.

Your purpose and passion go hand in hand because remember Purpose is your WHY mixed with your WHAT. Purpose is why you were created and what you were created to do. Your passion is what is the driving force behind what you do?

The great thing about passion is it is full of momentum, energy, life, and hope! Your passion will keep you going when you come across a few no's, when you were expecting to hear YES! Your passion will keep going when you know for certain that you are operating in your life purpose, doing exactly what our Creator placed you on this earth to do!

How I Launched My Business

Here's what I didn't understand…. when I wrote and published my first book, that is the day I launched my business as an entrepreneur. You are in business when you have a product or service in which you offer in exchange for currency.

Here I had written this great book that was selling like hot cakes and Amazon was paying me royalties every month for allowing me to sell my book on their website. I was also selling my book on my personal website where I was receiving 100% commission because I was not going through a third party.

What is one thing you can do *now* to bring in money residually (repeatedly)? List below.

What is holding you back from doing what you wrote above?

If fear wasn't an option, what would you do professionally?

After writing my book and celebrating it being on the Amazon Best Sellers list as well as becoming a National Best-Selling Author, I began to also create YouTube videos where I would develop a topic and teach on it. I also began to get out and speak more sharing my story with anyone who would offer me a platform which gave me an opportunity to minister to hurting people.

Amid continuing to blog, promote my book, conducting what I used to call *Empowerment Calls* and accepting speaking engagements here are some things I always kept in mind that I recommend you do as well:

1. Be true to who you are. People can spot a fake!

2. OWN your story and never be ashamed of it. If you did it, free yourself by talking about it. In return you'll free others.

3. Clear out your space of small thinkers. Small thinking and negative speaking are contagious!

4. Refuse to give up until YOU WIN! Giving up is not an option therefore, you must experience what I call a *Mindset Preset* where you preset your mind to winning mode while declaring: *"All I do is WIN!"*

5. Share your story authentically and un-apologetically with a goal in mind of not only empowering your listeners but helping them draw strength from you as you speak.

Strategies to Sharing Your Story

When sharing your story, the #1 thing I recommend is that you first be sure you are healed before sharing. I witnessed someone share her story prematurely and she literally cried the entire time she was up sharing, and I knew instantly this wasn't the time for her to share it.

Now, you may be saying, you drew that conclusion simply because she was crying, Carla? No, it was her level of confidence, her choice words, and her demeanor. I knew she was still currently in a battle that God had not *yet* brought her through but for some reason an opportunity was presented for her to speak, and she accepted, which in return I feel did more damage *to* her than it worked *for* her.

Which brings me to my next point…

#2: Be careful about sharing your story before the appointed time.

We must understand that before we can help others, we must first help ourselves. Timing matters and when it's time you'll know. No, you don't have to be perfect, but there should be a specific destination or journey you should desire to take the person listening to.

This book is not your ordinary book on business. I know I named it *The Entrepreneur Blueprint,* however, I must be honest that it has literally shifted right now as I write this book at 4:30 a.m. This is a book on how I have taken my *real-life* experiences that have caused me the most embarrassment, hurt, pain and agony and transformed my storm into a story, my mess into a movement and my pain into profit! Guess what? You can too but you must be willing to be vulnerable, honest with yourself and honest with the world. Too many are pretending to have perfect lives in hopes of gaining "likes" and "shares" on social media. What people need nowadays is someone who understands their struggle and how you overcame, or perhaps how you function daily with a thorn in your side!

I do believe that timing in all things is essential to being effective and operating in our divine purpose. There are times we are waiting on God but then there are also times when Holy Spirit has given us the go ahead to share our story, or to begin to mentor and coach others but we allow fear to cripple us and literally suck the life out of our bodies that prevent us from reaching our full potential and completing our assignment here on the earth.

I can remember the first time I shared my story. I was extremely nervous and to prove it I had literally wrote down my testimony and read it word for word to the audience. Now that was over five years ago. Today I can speak from my heart because my testimony has become real to me. God and I have been through some things together, and my love and passion for Him has intensified therefore, while sharing my story I no longer need notes like I used to. My heart is full of so much love for Him that I am able to share without reading verbatim off of a sheet of paper.

Don't believe me? Go to my YouTube channel, Carla Cannon (be sure to subscribe to it) and you will see my first video ever when I was sharing my testimony at a church. I had on a teal shirt with a black skirt. Guess what else? I wasn't fully delivered yet, but I was in my process of overcoming and I too was one who shared my story too soon. Be careful how you allow people within the church to push you out into purpose before preparing you for the warfare that comes along with it.

How to Know When You Are Ready to Share

I am not sure if I can teach this part, but I will do my best. How to know when you are ready to share your story is when you have weathered the storms that come along with the process. You are no longer falling over what once held you bound. You are no longer angry or harboring un-forgiveness, but you are truly free.

Some of the most powerful testimonies (or stories) I've heard were of the likes of Oprah Winfrey, Tyler Perry, Tony Robbins, Mary Kay Ash, Les Brown, Steve Harvey; etc. These individuals have phenomenal stories of how they started out with nothing or how they too had labels placed on them and how they overcame.

One thing is certain, the best time to share your story is when you are no longer in that same place. Once you are speaking from the pureness of your heart and have withstood all the tests and trials and are no longer dipping and dodging in and out of the very thing you are saying Christ has redeemed you from.

Now don't be alarmed but the adversary will come to tempt you after you open your mouth telling the world what the Lord has done for you. If you happen to fall, dust yourself off, identify how you got there (what doors you left open) and get right back in the ring. Don't allow the adversary to beat you down and make you feel that your voice no longer matters because you messed up.

As a woman in ministry, I have had tons of screw ups but guess what? I refused to allow my issues or storms in life to keep me down. Each time I'd slip and fall, I'd get right back up to the point that I had to re-establish some boundaries and come to grips with the fact of whatever it took for me to *get* free, it would take that plus more for me to *stay* free.

I refuse to sell you false hope or share a watered-down testimony, but the truth is it is going to be hard, but you can do it! Whenever you share your testimony of overcoming drug addiction, pornography, being a cutter, nicotine addiction; etc. you will be tempted to pick those habits back up again.

It's natural after a heartache or stressful moments to revert to our previous lifestyles but we must declare that our past has nothing we want! Now press forward!

The Correlation of Pain & Purpose

The great thing about pain is that it never enters our life without having a divine purpose. Everything I dealt with in my life from a child to current was all for my good. Because of all I've encountered I have been able to create the following products:

1. **Breaking the Cycle of Fear**- Teaching people how to rid themselves of fear and operate in courage by stepping outside of their comfort zones

2. **Defining the Pearl in You** – Helping women identify their life purpose by first leading them into a deeper relationship with Christ which is the ultimate confidence booster.

3. **Write the Book Already**- Where I teach others how to write a best-selling book in 7 days using a system that prevents writer's block forever!

4. **Fire Your Boss & Hire Yourself as COO**- I am sharing 6 steps on how to transition off your job into full time entrepreneurship. And more!

The great thing about life is there is no such thing as a wasted experience. However, you can choose the route of fear or the route of courage. I chose the route of courage and so can you!

My definition of courage is: The power and ability to move forward in the very presence of fear without acknowledging its presence which diminishes its power.

The only reason I was able to write books such as The Power in Waiting and A Single Woman's Focus is because I was not afraid to be vulnerable and expose my shortcomings to help prevent others from making the same mistakes I made. This is key in using your pain to transform the lives of others…. you must be willing to be vulnerable and share even the things you were once embarrassed about. You can't be concerned with your naysayers or even individuals who share your last name. If God leads you to share your story, I encourage you to do so and not think twice about it.

Your pain has tremendous purpose that you have no idea about because often we are blinded by our current circumstance that limits us from being forward thinkers. Never in a million years would I have thought that a southern girl such as myself who grew up with so many odds against her would be filled with so many dreams and visions that only God Himself could manifest in her life. I'm telling you; I've had to pray my way through some of life's most difficult moments. I've had to walk alone. I've had to endure being lied on, overlooked, rejected, and even abandoned in order to reach my place in destiny. I've had to disconnect from some of my best friends (or so I thought) all because God was changing who I was as a person and those who surrounded me at that time were causing more harm than good.

Now is the time to get comfortable with being uncomfortable.

For you to tap into your purpose by first identifying your passion, you must be willing to change your connections and fill your circle with individuals who are smarter than you, make more money than you, and whose names are bigger than yours. Will it make you uncomfortable? Absolutely! But that is an enabler for you soaring!

Stepping out of your comfort zone is a major requirement if you are going to be a world changer or trailblazer! You must become someone others admire and desire to follow. Believe it or not you already are you just don't know it yet.

Quotes on Passion:

According to www.INC.com they describe passion as the following:

Passion is the energy that keeps us going, that keeps us filled with meaning, happiness, excitement, and anticipation. Passion is a powerful force in accomplishing anything you set your mind to, and in fully experiencing work and life possibilities.

"Every great dream begins with a dreamer. Always remember, you have within you the strength, the patience, and the passion to reach for the stars to change the world." -Harriet Tubman

"There is no passion to be found playing small--in settling for a life that is less than the one you are capable of living." -Nelson Mandela

"Develop a passion for learning. If you do, you will never cease to grow." -Anthony J. D'Angelo

"Passion is energy. Feel the power that comes from focusing on what excites you." -Oprah

"If passion drives you, let reason hold the reins." -Benjamin Franklin

"You have to be burning with an idea, or a problem, or a wrong that you want to right. If you're not passionate enough from the start, you'll never stick it out." - Steve Jobs

"If you feel like there's something out there that you're supposed to be doing, if you have a passion for it, then stop wishing and just do it." -Wanda Sykes

"Find what you are passionate about, and it will lead to your life purpose." - Carla R. Cannon

Chapter 3
Developing Your Gift into a Thriving Business

Do you believe it is possible to get paid to do something you truly enjoy doing? For so long we have settled for jobs we hated, only to work for a boss who doesn't truly value who we are in exchange for a check that barely meets our basic needs.

Now, perhaps you are someone who loves your job but desire to build your own brand and business. This too is possible, however; part time entrepreneur life and full-time entrepreneur life are operated off two totally different frequencies.

As a part time entrepreneur, you are tempted to put in only half the effort because you still have your 9 to 5 check to rely on. However, as a full-time entrepreneur it is important that you be 100% invested in this new unconventional path that hundreds if not thousands of people only dream of doing, if only they had the courage.

When I decided to leave my job on October 15, 2014, I had to make a commitment to be fully invested in the road I was about to embark upon. However, my level of commitment did not take place on that day. Prior to then I had spent the two and a half previous years building my following, developing a brand, and establishing my voice using outlets such as social media, YouTube and hosting my own events.

I didn't wait on anyone to provide a platform for me, but I utilized opportunities that were provided to me and began where I was, using what I had. I have hosted dozens of events from workshops to conferences and written various books that I am extremely proud of. Not to mention the favor I gained in 2014 by being invited to cover media at Bishop T.D. Jakes' Woman Thou Art Loosed Conference in Atlanta, GA. That was a weekend that changed my life forever.

I was later invited as a guest on BRAVO's Reality TV Star, Jewel Tankard (wife of the legendary Ben Tankard/from hit show Thicker Than Water) television show, *The Jewel Tankard Show* that aired on IMPACT Network in over three million homes.

All of this was within a five-year time frame and I am literally just getting started. I have been blessed to share the stage with some of today's influential leaders such as Dr. Yvonne Capehart, Jekalyn Carr (who used to write for the Youth Column in my magazine, Women of Standard), Real Talk Kim, Tera C. Hodges, and Jewel Tankard (just to name a few.)

I established a movement, Women of Standard, where for two years I operated as Chief Editor of a magazine where I featured and exclusively interviewed some of the greatest pioneers in Gospel such as Dr. Jamal Bryant (for our Men of Standard column), Dr. Traci Lynn (Founder of Traci Lynn Fashion Jewelry), Stormie Omartian, Vashawn Mitchell, Tasha Cobbs, Dr. Stacia Pierce, Dr. T.L. Penny, Yolanda Adams, Kierra Sheard and many more!

Why am I sharing all of this? Because I want you to know and understand that it is possible to profit from your pain if you would get serious about your life and identify what it is you *really* want.

I encourage you to get in a quiet space and be real with yourself by 1.) Confronting your issues, 2.) Healing from your pain 3.) Embracing the process of transformation and 4.) Be willing to help someone else overcome as well or even prevent them from dealing with all you've had to face.

Many people like to focus on intervention while my preference personally is prevention. If I can prevent a teenage girl from losing her virginity to a guy who cares nothing about her, I'd rather do that than share strategies on how to raise a child as a teenage mom. I'm all for *preventing* my brothers and sisters from falling in the same ditches and dry places I once found myself in.

Before you can develop a thriving business, you must first identify what your gift is. After years of soul searching, praying and snotting over various altars I finally came to grips with the fact that I am a writer and a speaker. There is no greater joy I find than sitting at my laptop writing books or creating mastermind projects and resources to add value to the lives of others.

One of the ways I developed my gift into a thriving business was by 1. Recognizing I had a voice that others needed to hear and 2. Learning that I was a necessary vessel, and my experiences (successes and failures) were not for me to keep to myself but to share with others along the way.

Once you learn that you are a person of value, you will stop second guessing yourself, doubting your ability and will no longer compare yourself to others. I used to be the same way, trust me. The voices of previous teachers and family members rehearsed in my head for years until I snatched out the plug and turned a deaf ear to all that garbage! I used to compare myself to other women who were making greater impact (or so I thought) because they could host a packed-out event and I would do great to get 100 people to show up. Now notice what I just said, *"I would do great to get 100 people to show up."* As if having that number to show up was an easy task.

When you compare yourself to others you rob yourself of your true ability and you diminish your power. You also rob yourself of your joy and inner peace while presenting failure as an option before you ever begin. I remember seeing women I admired host events and have some of the biggest named people to show up as their keynote speaker and I'd be like wow! I want to do that!

But here's what I learned: it's not about the person who shows up, it's about the value they bring. I would support and endorse these women while having a blind eye that I was literally paying for their programs when I could teach what they were teaching. I would pay money to support their events, but they never paid a dime, sowed an offering, or even became a sponsor for any of mine.

I learned rather quickly that being a woman in my thirties I was identified as the new kid on the block because it was almost like I appeared out of nowhere and no one had a chance to prepare for my arrival.

What do I mean? One day there was no Carla Cannon. The next it was, "Who's that lady?" (Yes, I wrote that with the sound of Isley Brothers in my head-Ha!) Sadly, I was viewed as a threat to others (not all but some) in my community as well as some I had grown to admire. You can imagine the level of pain and rejection I felt because here I was still trying to find my way, still comparing myself to others when all along others could see what I possessed but it hadn't yet registered with me.

I remember a previous coach telling me, *"Girl you just popped up on the scene and in a huge way! You about to make a lot of the veterans mad!"* He went on to say, *"Your branding is tight, your message is impactful, and your marketing is on point."* He then said, *"Get ready for the hate!"*

Now, me being a newbie I was thinking what a great way to encourage me as your client but boy was he right. I began to get the cold shoulder from women who saw me not as their sister but as their competitor.

Personally, I don't believe anyone out there is my competitor or yours either. For what God has for each of us is for us! I know many people who like McDonald's that also like

Burger King. Those who like Jordan also like Kobe and LeBron. Those who enjoy Essence magazine also purchase Ebony and so on.

What's my point in all of this? Be aware that success comes with a price. It can be lonely at times, but you must constantly remind yourself that every part of your process is worth it. Everything from the bad business deals to the unsuccessful turnouts of your events; etc. That is one of the things I admire about Media Mogul, Tyler Perry. He tried for years (I believe over ten years) hosting play after play only to have a small group of people to show up. He continued and eventually had 300 people to attend in which he said he knew every one of them. Being a woman of vision, I understand his process because when I hosted my first event and didn't know half of the people there (and 250 people showed up) I was so in awe of God because that's how I knew it was Him moving on my behalf and not me in my own power and might.

Most of the events I host women travel from across the globe to attend and I have finally learned to be okay with that. I have also learned that I do not always have to be on the scene. There are some people you meet where you see them literally everywhere.

One thing I admire and love about Gospel Artist, Tamala Mann is she is exclusive. You cannot attend a local event and just see her there sitting on the third row. This is how she can charge over $25,000 for appearances because she is a rare gem that you can't come across on a daily basis.

Now am I saying walk around acting like you all that? Absolutely not! But what I am saying is that the more exclusive you become the more valuable you become to others. Many Christians are still walking around trying to be *all* things to *all* people. The problem with that is, we are not called to everyone. We each have what I call a remnant that we are called to reach by being who we are unapologetically. We do not have to scheme and connive others to join our team, but they will naturally be drawn to us.

In essence, all I am trying to say is-- a place of familiarity can be a very dangerous zone especially as an entrepreneur. It's okay to show up and support others but be sure to make your presence impactful. Don't just go places because you want to be seen. Allow Christ to be your PR (publicist) and as you remain low-key, he will release your name into Heaven which will transfer here on earth.

I've learned to guard my anointing and protect my gift and you must do the same. Now on the flip side of this I have been called stuck up and non-supportive. But neither are true. I used to get caught up in a lot of foolishness and nonsense as a younger woman (especially at religious functions…go figure) therefore, I've learned to keep my hips at home unless Holy Spirit releases me to go. If I don't receive clearance, I don't go. People can call me what they want. If it's not about purpose, Carla is not coming. I am learning to be a true imitator of Christ and how He always said, *"I only do what I see the father do."* (John 5:19- NLT)

That is the place you must grow to where you no longer care what others think of you or have to say about you but you are laser focused on hearing God's voice so you can follow His instructions.

Getting Down to the Nitty Gritty

In order for you to enter into full time entrepreneurship you must first be able to replace your current income. I also recommend that you begin to build your business while working your 9 to 5 because your current income can not only help you save money but also help you fund your vision.

Write out below what type of business you desire to launch.

_____
_____
_____
_____
_____
_____
_____

Who do you desire to service? (Who is your target market?)

_____
_____
_____

How do you plan to make money?

_____
_____
_____

What products will you create, or services will you offer to generate income and how much will it be?

Product:	Price:
1.	$
2.	$
3.	$
4.	$

After you have identified how you plan to replace your current income you must then develop systems (operations) which we will go into detail in Chapter 6.

Systems are simply how you desire your business to be ran. The below factors are important for you to know as an entrepreneur:

- Branding is how you get KNOWN

- Marketing is how you get FOUND

- Sales is how you get PAID

- Operations is how you BUILD A BUSINESS

To run a successful business, it is important that you educate yourself on all 4 of the above points. According to Entrepreneur.com *branding* is defined as: *"The marketing practice of creating a name, symbol or design that identifies and differentiates a product from other products.*

Entrepreneur.com goes on to say, *"Simply put, your brand is your promise to your customer. It tells them what they can expect from your products and services, and it differentiates your offering from that of your competitors. Your brand is derived from who you are, who you want to be and who people perceive you to be."*

Many people think your brand is simply your awesome or unique logo, web design and how well your business cards look. But that couldn't be the furthest from the truth. Your brand is as Entrepreneur.com mentioned above, who you are, who you desire to be and who others perceive you to be.

Take myself for instance, when I first started out, I was unsure of all those things. All I knew was that I was a woman who had been hurt, had a painful past and managed not to lose my mind in the process and I wanted to help others do the same thing.

Before we step out and do anything it is vital that we become healed for real. Past hurts can ruin or even prevent kingdom relationships and connections. Know that in order to overcome a thing you must first identify that it exists because it is impossible to conquer what we are unwilling to confront. We also can't confront what we are unwilling to identify.

In the words of Iyanla Vanzant, "You must be willing to do your work!" This is so true because before you can help anyone else you must first rescue *you!*

Once you experience healing you can move forward with identifying what your gifts, talents and abilities are. Let's jump into this below:

Take a moment and write down 5 things you have to offer to the world.

1._____

2._____

3._____

4._____

5._____

Prior to being branded as *Carla R. Cannon, The Trailblazer (where my mission is to equip, build and strengthen women from the pulpit to the marketplace on how to operate authentically and un-apologetically in their divine calling with a spirit of excellence)* I had no clue the power or anointing that resided within me. All I knew was when I opened my mouth to speak; people listened.

I began my journey as I mentioned previously sending encouraging texts daily to every number in my phone. I did that for years, and then I began a newsletter which later developed into a magazine which today has become a global movement where I am on a mission to make Jesus famous and help others identify and operate in their life's purpose before it's too late.

But guess what? My transitional moment occurred the day I literally owned my pain and made a decision to stand on top of it. I stopped talking around my issues and disappointments and faced them. I owned them. Once I accepted that those things did in fact happen to me, I began to speak to my hurt, pain and fears reminding them they have no victory over me. I began to snatch back my life, one by one. God began to peel back the layers, healing me one situation at a time. Today, I still have scars but instead of allowing them to hold me captive I share them with the world not from the place of a victim but as a victor because we are in fact more than conquerors! (Romans 8:37)

The day I decided to pen my pain is the day my life changed forever. *The Power in Waiting* was the book God used as my launching pad introducing my voice to the world!

What is your launching pad? How can you share your story with the world? I have an idea that I implement in my business daily. I teach a system which originated from my personal path and share how others can write their book and in return launch their business as an entrepreneur!

Writing a book is the best thing I could have ever done. It expanded my audience, provided me with global reach where others in Trinidad, UK, Germany, and more were purchasing my books from Amazon.com.

How did I do this? Instead of focusing on my book being the brand, I acknowledged that I am the brand. Whether I am writing books or operating as a minister or entrepreneur; all of it is me. It's who I am. I had to recognize that I am a walking brand and billboard (for Jesus) therefore, with that comes major pressure and responsibility as well accountability.

I said all of this to say, get your mind off a logo, and how to build a business and start with first building YOU. Build yourself up as a person, an innovator, a world changer, a motivator, an encourager! Know that whatever it is you desire to be or do you can! The only limits that exist are the ones you place on yourself!

Next, marketing is how you are found. For me to sell tons of books and become identified as a National Best-Selling Author I had to not be afraid to put myself out there. What do I mean by this? I was blogging daily, sharing empowering and uplifting posts on Facebook and Twitter. I took the time to find inspirational pictures to compliment the messages I had to share on Instagram. I utilized outlets such as YouTube and began to record myself every time I went out to speak.

Key Point: As a speaker, it is important to record yourself every time you speak publicly!

Another social media outlet that is very popular right now is Periscope and if you create a free katch.me account they will store all your videos for you which allows you to then go back and upload them on your YouTube channel.

If you go to my YouTube channel right now: or by searching Carla Cannon, you will see my Periscope videos listed under: Daily Trailblazing Moments by Carla Cannon. These are simply videos I conducted live via Periscope, which is an app that enables you to speak live to your audience from across the globe. They can see and hear you, but you can only read the messages they put on the screen.

So basically, what I'm saying is in order to develop a thriving business you must not be afraid to be seen, be heard and be known.

Next is sales! Sales is how you get paid. Simply put to be able to leave your job and operate as a business owner you must first be able to replace the income you make on your job.

In my Fire Your Boss & Hire Yourself as COO Self-Study Program I share a step-by-step process which involves developing what I call, an EXIT Plan. This plan includes two different types of budgets: A Survival Budget and A Thriving Budget. For greater detail be sure to check out this great offer at www.CarlaCannon.com.

You are not in business if you are not making money. If you love what you do so much that you desire to do it free, then that my friend is a hobby and I wish more power to you! But that is not my desire nor my focus. It is impossible to fund the kingdom or take care of your family if you are broke! (Okay, let me calm down.)

In my transition into full time entrepreneurship, I had to quickly learn that I had to rid my calendar of non-productive activities and focus more on what I call Revenue Producing Activities.

For example, a non-productive activity could be spending an hour on Facebook scrolling through looking at what everyone else is doing. Or spending 45 minutes watching the hit show, *Empire* when I didn't make time that day to work on building my own empire.

However, a revenue producing activity could be spending 15 minutes on the phone with a client who is inquiring about my publishing company, Cannon Publishing and ends up choosing one of my packages. Then the call ends with her giving me her credit card number to secure payment.

Another revenue producing activity could be spending time creating a project or mastermind that will lead me to financial increase. Revenue producing activities may not bring you money the exact same day, but it leads you to it. Does that make sense? Meaning you must be intentional in everything you do and be aware of time stealers and vision killers.

Be aware of the hellophone. Yes, I meant hell-o-phone because so many people spend time lying and gossiping than being productive then wonder why they make zero progress in life. There are some people who are designed to be a distraction in your life and that is why it's vital that you give every person you are currently connected to a place. Either they have a place of significance because they add value to your life, or they hold a place of insignificance because they add zero value to your life. Only you can decide who they are and what box you will place them in.

Author Sophia Nelson talks about knowing your *front row* in her book, *The Woman Code.* I advise every woman to read this book for it will literally transform how you operate personally and professionally.

Note: People will enter and exit our lives all the time, but it's up to us to identify why they showed up and whether they are a temporary or permanent connection. The latter is often hard to determine, however, time will reveal all things.

Lastly, there are systems of operations which is simply how you run your business. My recommendation is to set everything up on automation so that if you are sick or have an important meeting to attend you can make money in your sleep.

Here is an example of a system. Mary Jo visits www.CarlaCannon.com and she is highly intrigued by my exclusive Fire Your Boss & Hire Yourself as COO Self-Study Program. Therefore, she makes the investment and upon receipt she immediately receives a notification in her email personally from me thanking her for purchasing my program and includes Module I for her to get started right away.

The automatic message Mary Jo received is called an autoresponder in which my web developer set up so my business could run on its own while I am out spending time with my daughter, or at a lunch meeting with a potential client.

Then over the next three weeks Mary Jo will receive Modules II-IV directly to her email and I never had to speak with her simply because she saw what she wanted, paid for it and I had the proper system set up to accommodate her needs in an instantaneous manner. This my friend is what we call "the power of automation."

Remembering that you are your brand, not being afraid to be seen, heard, and known, focusing on revenue producing activities while watching out for time stealers and vision killers all while setting up a profitable business using systems and operations will better position you to be a successful entrepreneur.

Chapter 4
Mistakes Aspiring Entrepreneurs Make

Now that you have heard my story of how I entered full time entrepreneurship I decided to also reach out to others in various industries to share their story as well common mistakes aspiring *and* established entrepreneurs make.

The women who reached out to the response of me seeking entrepreneurs to collaborate with me on this book project are amazing and are successful in their own right. They are fierce, focused, and fabulous while they continue to thrive and operate in their divine calling!

Including the story of these women was not a financial gain for me; as a matter of fact, I did not charge them a dime but rather viewed it as an opportunity to display true, authentic sisterhood. I know others who have done book collaborations and charged people crazy amounts of money to share their story and pearls of wisdom but that was not the avenue I was led or even desired to take.

Truth of the matter is the fact that each of these ladies chose to be a part of this book and in doing so it provided greater value to you as the reader.

In an effort to further empower, equip and encourage you while in pursuit of your entrepreneurial journey, I intentionally sought-after women who have experienced success and failure (which were actually blessings in disguise) along their journey. This was done to show you that dreams are indeed real, and you will gain a few bumps and bruises along the way, but you must be determined to keep moving forward. No matter what refuse to give up on an opportunity to be able to dream with your eyes wide open!

Get ready to meet these amazing women and I encourage you to connect with them on social media such as Periscope, Facebook, Instagram, LinkedIn & Twitter. Do not be afraid to reach out and tell these women how their stories may have blessed you.

It's never easy to pen your pain or even your process for those are your private failures that honestly without the unction of Holy Spirit I'm sure many of us would not share. So, don't just read their story and be so quick to flip over to the next page. Know that these are *real* women, with *real* stories who are now experiencing *real* success who have decided to share their pearls of wisdom with you to help avoid any pitfalls that may be on your road to success.

I do not believe that life is the best teacher. I believe that life should be more about prevention than focusing on intervention. If I can learn from someone along the way that will prevent me from falling in the same ditch they fell in and I'm sure like you, that information will be greatly appreciated. So again, be sure to connect with these ladies for they were once where you may currently be right now. Let's dive in!

Meet Sandra Mizell Chaney, Author, Speaker, Transformational Life & Business Coach who also offers Federal Grant coaching/training and promotes Fatherless Daughter Advocacy trainings and workshops. Below is her story of transitioning into full time entrepreneurship.

The Day I Said *Yes!*
"My Entrepreneurial Chronicles"

So, I've discovered that the entrepreneurial journey is not for the faint of heart. There are ups and downs, challenges, roadblocks, naysayers, and doubt. This list could go on and on. But how you handle your journey will determine if you will succeed. The day I turned in my resignation to my job was the start of a beautiful yet challenging journey. There were many times I questioned my "yes" and I've asked myself on many occasions, *"What were you thinking?"*

Earlier on in my journey I attempted to quit and go back to what I considered stability, a job. During one of those moments of weakness I received an email that read: *"The road to success is not straight. There is a curve called Failure, a loop called Confusion, speed bumps called Friends, red lights called Enemies, caution lights called Family. You will have flats called Jobs. But, if you have a spare called Determination, an engine called Perseverance, insurance called Faith, a driver called God, you will make it to a place called Success."*

One day I heard a voice telling me it's time for you to walk in your true purpose and destiny. I was at the church altar when I heard a voice telling me *"The time has come for you to leave your job and step out on faith."* I looked around to see who was standing around me. There were a few people around, however they were engaged in other conservations. So, I interrupted a few of them and asked, *"Did you hear that?"* Of course, they said, *"Hear what?"* I was beginning to think I had lost my mind, but I knew what I heard was for me.

The fear of stepping out and pursuing the purpose and plan God had laid out for me was utterly frightening. I left my job November 1, 2013, very afraid of the unknown. God did not leave me hanging though. When I told people what I was going to do they attempted to give me all the reasons why I shouldn't pursue this new path to entrepreneurship. Many of them said, *"You just got married six months ago." "Your husband will be angry." "You don't know what you are doing."* You name it, I heard it and I admit I made the mistake of listening to them because I was supposed to exit my job in August not November. But after the delay, I made a decision to listen to God. I did just that and developed an exit strategy. The funny thing is the job I had at the time became my first client. During that time, I was the Community Education Manager for a Battered Women's Shelter. I developed programs, curriculums, and workshops for the community on domestic violence. I also was the voice at the local shelter in the community educating others on domestic violence and the effects it has as well as how they could be a part of the healing process for those affected. What I did not realize is this was the steppingstone to my life's work as an entrepreneur, speaker, coach and author.

Well, those contracts lasted a few years and paid well. The mistake I made was I forgot to plant more seeds. Being my own boss meant I was also responsible for tilling the land and planting seeds. Fear creeped in along with feelings of failure and as if I had made the worst mistake of my life. Due to entertaining these feelings and emotions I admit I became stuck and found myself putting in applications, seeking employment again. Really God? I knew it was time for me to shut up and listen for what was next.

I pushed through my fear of failure by exchanging the negative opinions of others as well as my personal thoughts toward myself with what God's word said about me. I admit I didn't always succeed at this. But I kept moving forward anyway. I had many challenges on this journey financially, emotionally, and physically. Fear would creep in; stress was at high levels and emotionally I was struggling. Self-care was definitely out the window. I remembered what God said and kept moving. I started taking care of me, shutting out well-meaning voices and listening to God. The one thing I learned and became etched in the core of my soul is that the Kingdom of God is within. I do not need to look outside of myself or to others for what God has already planted inside of me.

So how did I push past my fear which was also disguised as procrastination, busy work, distractions, unworthiness, and a lack of confidence? I had to first acknowledge that the fear was there. You cannot change what you are unwilling to acknowledge. Secondly, I had to come to terms with the fact that I was holding me back. The Bible tells us in John 10:10 that the enemy comes to kill, steal, and destroy. Well, I had to acknowledge that the *real* enemy was me. This was a hard pill to swallow, yet necessary if I were to move forward. I made time to sit quietly, evaluate myself and listen to the voice of God.

I began asking God to show me, *me.* I needed to know what was holding me back. What Holy Spirit revealed was a lot of hurt, pain and un-forgiveness. I could feel all the negative words spoken over me by others. I could see how I was pretending to have it all together when I really did not. I saw all the ugliness that I originally did not want to see. What do you need to see in order to move forward? Just a question for you to ponder.

After seeing these things, which took a minute, I made the choice to forgive myself and those who hurt me. I decided it was no longer of value to hold on to these things. They were blocking my present and future. They had taken up space rent free way too long. I am a conqueror of domestic violence, sexual assault, homelessness, abandonment, and single parenting. It was time to act like it! Lastly, to shut down the voices, I began meditating on God's word more and more as well as wrote out affirmations and placed them everywhere in my home. I also created a vision board for my life which helped me tremendously.

I accepted my call to be a Compelling Change Agent, Certified Transformation Coach/ Speaker, Certified Fatherless Daughter Advocate and Best-Selling Author of three books. I believe my life's work is to help women live and love beyond their titles, be more than their businesses/ministries and transform their lives to manifest the vision they were created to bring forth. Through sharing my life experiences and lessons as a coach and speaker, I was fashioned by God to help you to take off the mask, heal your soul wounds, create a new chapter in your story and release the courage to love freely and authentically from the inside out.

As a fatherless daughter advocate, I help elevate the awareness of the negative impact that fatherlessness has on a female's life while teaching women and girls how to redefine who they are. We also focus on helping them reclaim their self-worth and rewrite a new narrative for their lives through "The Journey to Being Process™". Yup, my life's work; I still say yes, and I am very grateful!

Remember: *"The road to success is not straight. There is a curve called Failure, a loop called Confusion, speed bumps called Friends, red lights called Enemies, caution lights called Family. You will have flats called Jobs. But, if you have a spare called Determination, an engine called Perseverance, insurance called Faith, a driver called God, you will make it to a place called Success."* (Author Unknown)

As it relates to my own entrepreneurial journey, I have made a few mistakes and they are listed below. It is my hope that you will learn from my path and not cause them to make you stuck like it did me initially.

1. **Fear of failure:** Fear kept me stuck for a long time. Fear also had me thinking I was not good enough. Fear is the gateway to so many negative thoughts and will keep you locked up *if* you allow it. I changed my thoughts, daily routine and connected with coaches and mentors to help me free my mind from the inside/out.

2. **Fear of success:** Once I learned how to deal with fear of failure, fear of success began to creep in. Along with success comes naysayers, character attacks, negative comments etc. What I'm realizing is that all that stuff is not about me. It is about that person and how they are feeling about their success or perhaps the lack thereof. Now I smile, pray for them, and keep it moving.

3. **Listening to other well-meaning people:** Not trusting in what God said, I sought out the opinions of others. While the advice was good, it sometimes changed the direction of what God originally instructed me to do. This was a costly mistake. These mistakes taught me to tap in and seek God. The answers I needed were always there. Truth is, I trusted others more than I trusted the God in me which was my first mistake.

4. **Trying to be perfect - perfectionism:** This kept me from moving forward on many projects. I kept extending start dates or finding reasons to postpone. Perfectionism became my excuse. It had to be right, or it was not happening. What I learned is that nothing is ever perfect. Things can and will happen. It's how you respond to the challenges that determine your success in life. Just keep moving.

5. **Lack of self-care:** Everything I do now comes from a place of love. This was not always my stance. My cup always ran dry. I was in constant pursuit of trying to keep up with others instead of running my own race. I did not know how to love or put myself first. I put everyone else's problems, ideas, opinions, and pain before mine. I had to learn to fill my cup first which meant saying no instead of yes, place *me* on my own calendar (and keep the appointment), as well as set much needed boundaries.

In addition to making my own mistakes which I now know were simply learning opportunities, I have also witnessed others do the following:

1. **Failure to set attainable goals:** Entrepreneurs sometimes start putting their best foot forward without a plan of how to see the vision or dream manifest. Write out your goals and the steps to reach the goals so that the vision will manifest.

2. **Having too many distractions:** It is easy to have many ideas and forget the main purpose of your business. Multiple streams of income are great when you have a plan of execution. Stay focus and master the core of your business first. Otherwise, you will become a jack of all trades and a master of none.

3. **Failure to Respond Promptly:** Keeping your word speaks of your character. If you say you are going to respond within 24 – 48 hours, then do so. At the very least reach out to the client to let them know you received their message as

a courtesy. People don't spend money with unreliable people- keep that in mind.

4. **Chasing money:** As an entrepreneur it's easy to get caught up in chasing the dollar instead of flowing in your purpose. When you focus on what you love to do, the money will come. When you focus on the money you end up stressed out and wondering if you were called to do this. Stop chasing money and focus on your purpose.

5. **Thinking you got this:** Every entrepreneur needs a support team -- even if that team is simply your coach or mentor. You don't have all the answers. Having prayer warriors on your team is a plus!

Connect with Sandra Chaney today!
Facebook: Sandra Mizell Chaney
Twitter: @smchaney
Instagram: @transformationspecialist
www.SandraChaney.com

Meet Michelle Edelen, Founder of Excellence In All Consulting LLC. Michelle J. Edelen lives by her motto "always excel, never settle, excellence is the only option." As The Excellence Engineer™, Michelle is a coach, mentor, speaker and change catalyst for those who are ready to get to their "Place of Excellence™."

All in God's Timing

I have always had an entrepreneurial spirit. I have sold products at conferences, flea markets, trade shows and other events. I even sold frozen cups in my neighborhood as a child. None of these endeavors were successful for many different reasons. The reasons for my lack of success in my early entrepreneurial endeavors ranged from lack of resources to lack of understanding of how and where to begin to a basic lack of desire to make the businesses work.

Although I had a dream of being an entrepreneur, I pursued higher education because that's what was expected. That was the normal, preferred route. Get a degree. Get a job. Live happily ever after. I was quite successful taking this route. I found myself neck deep in employment in the wildly growing telecom industry. I was there during the days of milk and honey. I remember the 25% salary increases, the five-figure bonuses and the trips affectionately known as boondoggles! I remember the sales trips to Vegas, Miami, Tennessee and Toronto, Canada.

I was working a job that I liked and at which I excelled. After more than 15 years of riding the wave, I became complacent. I was stuck and I knew there was more for me to do. In June 2001, my husband and I purchased a new home. By August 2001, we had our third child. In October 2001, I was offered two options from my job (which honestly felt more like an ultimatum.) I was presented with the choice of either a.) Move to Guadalajara Mexico and keep my job or b.) Accept a severance package and be laid off.

The answer was pretty much a no-brainer. With a newborn baby, two elementary school aged children and a husband whose career was skyrocketing, moving to Mexico was not in the plan for my husband and me. So, I took the package. I found myself unemployed, with a brand-new baby during the time of one of the worst recessions in 20 years. By the grace of God and some generous angels here on earth, my husband and I made it through. We suffer some bumps and bruises, but we made it through.

Again, the entrepreneurial bug was biting at me continuously, but I didn't know where to begin. I started by assessing my skills and my education and then I identified what I enjoyed doing. I found public speaking to be my passion. But again, I didn't know where to begin. With few resources available and seeing no path to be the next "big name speaker", I did what I thought to be the next best thing. I found *another* job doing what brought me joy (or so I thought.) Although this job allowed me to do what I loved (speak and train others) it did not get me any closer to my desire to be an entrepreneur.

In 2012, I committed to growing my public speaking hobby into something more. I began to promote myself as much as I could, again without much direction or instruction. I had dreams of growing what I started into a full-time entrepreneurial endeavor.

I spent many hours trying to grow my business with varying levels of success.

By 2013, I had gained a bit of momentum and thought perhaps I could make this work. My level of confidence was increasing, and I was receiving more opportunities but most of them were for little or no pay. I knew two things at this point: One, there had to be a better way and two, I needed to expand to more than public speaking. I began to research the field of coaching and found that I was doing a good bit of coaching without a model, without any training and most importantly, without getting paid.

2013 was a year of growth for me. I began to invest in myself and my consulting practice regularly. I stepped out on faith in the face of fear and uncertainty and continued to push forward. I gained a level of momentum that has continued to push me to this day. I hired my first coach and continued to perfect my speaking skills.

I am so proud of Excellence in All Consulting LLC. It has grown each year and so have I. There are still challenges that I experience as an entrepreneur, but I am up for each of them. I will not shrink back from my calling for this opportunity is extremely rewarding and worth every hiccup I've ever experienced.

As it relates to my own entrepreneurial journey, I have made a few mistakes myself and have listed them below:

1. **Mistake:**   Waiting for perfection.

   Solution: I realized I didn't have to be perfect to move forward.

   Details: Perfection is not what is needed to excel in life. What is needed to move forward is obedience. I had to take myself by the collar and say, *"Michelle, you will either be obedient to God, or you will be disobedient to*

God. Which will it be?" As this question left my head and went to my lips. I still didn't move. When this question left my lips and went to my ears, I knew what the answer had to be.

In my head, I had every excuse as to why I could not move forward. All the excuses were perfectly lined up and ready to be shared with anyone who asked.

But when the answer and their accompanying excuses hit my ears and I heard what I had been inwardly saying to God, I had to repent. For me, Excellence in All Consulting, LLC is a God-ordained endeavor that will manifest in the marketplace. I could not disobey my creator.

However, I was still stuck on the word *perfect.* As I studied this in the Word of God (The Holy Bible), I found that what Christ refers to as perfect is actually maturity in him. I knew that through word study and pursuing a more intimate relationship with him I could develop into a greater level of maturity.

Then I had to ask God why this was so important in business. That's when I gained the revelation that Excellence in All Consulting, LLC would be a direct representation of all he already had me doing in the ministry.

This was an Ah-Ha moment for me that opened me up to a whole new world. I finally realized that ministry and marketplace could co-exist, and I no longer had to choose which one to operate in. Now many people may have gotten to this place sooner than me. What matters is that God got me there.

I began a personal journey of understanding the business owners of the Bible and their characteristics. In particular, I grew fond of Lydia. What I came to understand is that her business afforded her the ability to own a large home. She used her home to offer a resting place for Paul, Timothy, Luke, and Silas. Therefore, her home was large enough to accommodate her family and four visitors. Her business success was not just for the good of her along with her family, but it was for the good of the kingdom.

For me, this is why perfection – maturity in Christ is so critical. I have to be ready to offer my success in service to the kingdom. Once I grasped this point in my mind, heart, and soul I moved forward.

2. Mistake: Paralyzed by fear.

  Solution: PRAY AND STUDY THE WORD!!!!!!!!!!!

Details: I believe the enemy uses fear most effectively against God's children. He works to paralyze us with fear in an effort to stop what we have been predestined to do. I fell so deeply into this trap until it is almost embarrassing. I knew my answer was in God's word.

I studied one scripture until it became my mantra – *""So do not fear, for I am with you; do not be dismayed, for I am your God. I will strengthen you and help you; I will uphold you with my righteous right hand." (Isaiah 41:10 (NIV)*

I found that my fear was born out of a place of perceived weakness. For some odd reason, as it related to my entrepreneurial journey, I felt weak.

I realize now that I was weak in a couple of areas. First, I was spiritually weak. I didn't have Isaiah 41:10 deeply rooted in my very being so when a perceived failure hit, I was shaken. Instead of relying on God and his power,

I was trying to strengthen myself. In other words, I was trying to be this super entrepreneur on my own. I had gotten ahead of God and that is an uncomfortable place to be. Being in this state left me vulnerable to the other area of weakness I experienced.

The second area of weakness was emotionally. I was so in my feelings! I can look back now and chuckle but during that time, my emotions were intense. I took everything personally and responded from that same place. I was quick to become disappointed, hurt, and offended. I took every 'no' as an indictment on Michelle. My emotional state caused me to make everything about me.

The odd part is that I was only this way as it related to my business. I wasn't this way in my ministry, my career, with my family, friends, etc. This emotional sensitivity only surfaced when it was a matter related to my business. I knew it was a trick of the enemy because I have never in my life felt this way until I stepped out on faith to become an entrepreneur.

I studied this scripture and I prayed it back to God. I quoted it to myself and never let it slip far from my mind. This scripture was my portion. I heavily relied upon it.

3. **Mistake:**   Focusing on your current lack of resources.

   Solution: Start with what you have.

   Details: I found as many free tools as I could. It's amazing what's available to you for free if you will seek it out. I joined mailing lists for different coaches, authors, consultants, etc. I joined various Facebook groups and learned as much as I could.

   Simultaneously, I looked at the household budget to see where I could cut my expenditures. I quickly found that one less trip to the hair and nail salon and more brown bag lunch days per week could easily fund a class for me to sharpen my skills. The bottom line is you have to reprioritize. Just ask yourself, *"What is most important?"* The answer to this question for me was Excellence in All Consulting, LLC!

4. **Mistake:**   Not having a coach.

Solution: Hire a coach, quickly!

Details: Fortunately, I came to understand the necessity of having a coach early on in my entrepreneurial journey. I find it hard to articulate all that changed for me once I hired a coach.

First, I had in a coach someone who understood and spoke my language. Several years ago, I struggled to find anyone who understood what I needed; what I was trying to do, etc. When I hired my first coach, she was able to help me focus by asking the right questions (many of which I had no answer). As we continued to work together, I found my level of clarity increasing.

Next, hiring a coach thrust me into an accountability zone that I had not experienced in my consulting practice. If I said I would do something, then I was held to it with little to no exception. I found this to be extremely helpful.

Finally, having a coach helped increase my coaching skills. I learned from watching the process. I learned from all the activities, worksheets, etc. that were given to me. I was like a sponge. I used every conversation, session, live event, etc. with my coach as an opportunity to grow as a better overall person and professional coach.

5. **Mistake:** Not fully understanding my target market.

Solution: RESEARCH! RESEARCH! RESEARCH!

Details: I totally abandoned all my education on this step. I have no idea why. In B-school, we learned that the rule is RESEARCH! RESEARCH! RESEARCH! I, for some reason, thought it did not apply to becoming an entrepreneur. I was certain I knew who my target market was, what they looked like, where they shopped, what they ate and of course, what they wanted. I skipped this very critical part of the process.

Skipping this part of the process proved to be problematic in many ways. I became frustrated. I lost money. I wasted time. I almost gave up. I had to stop and go back to this step. I found that I could not take my consulting practice any further until I corrected this one thing.

Once I built an avatar of my target client, I quickly realized that I had been doing many things wrong. For example, I was on the wrong social media platforms. I was on Facebook, Pinterest, Twitter, Instagram, etc. because I thought I had to be. But I realized my target market was not found on all those platforms. To be honest, once I scaled back from some of the social media platforms, I felt relieved. You should have seen me trying to manage all those pages and at that time I hadn't heard of social media chunking tools. I was actually posting to each of them individually. When I look back on it, I see just how ill-informed I was.

Now I'm on the social media platforms that work for my client-base and it is working well. I still have much to learn but I'm seeing much better results. My stress level as it relates to my target market is considerably lower than it was.

Here are the mistakes I have witnessed other entrepreneurs make:

1. **Mistake:**   Great presentation but no content.

   Solution: Understand your "why" first. Your "why" will drive your content to a larger degree.

   Details: I've seen entrepreneurs who spend huge amounts of money to build a gorgeous website, beautiful social media presence, professional photos, etc. They put excessive amounts of energy and resources into their outer package. When it's time to engage a client, they have no foundational content and no program model/system to use. This leaves the entrepreneur to have to wing it. It is similar to a person who can talk their way into and out of any situation but when pressed can offer no detail. They are good at hypothesizing and pontificating but are never really able to fully answer a question or explain a program with specific detail. Again, this leaves the entrepreneur to have to wing it and it makes them appear unprepared.

2. **Mistake:**   Not fully understanding their target market.

   Solution: RESEARCH! RESEARCH! RESEARCH!

   Details: I have noticed that some entrepreneurs seem to take the scatter-shot approach. They shoot out a little of this and a little of that to see what sticks. When you view their social media or website, you can't tell what they really offer and more importantly, to whom it is offered. Their offerings seem disjointed and fragmented. Again, the approach seems to be one where the entrepreneur builds what they *think* their target market wants without doing the proper research to see who their target market is and what their pain points are.

I myself have been guilty of this mistake. I didn't take the time initially to really understand my target market from every angle. I found myself clientless and frustrated. Once I went back and completed this very important step, it made my life as an entrepreneur much easier and less stressful. It also helped me stop wasting money (that I didn't have!).

3. **Mistake:**   Circumventing the process.

Solution: Refuse to allow yourself to bypass or skip parts of the process.

Details: First, there is so much to be learned by going through the different stages of the process to becoming an entrepreneur. For example, if you don't complete the process of researching your target market and understanding their wants, needs, desires, etc. then you'll never understand why you built "it" but fail to attract the right clients.

Second, there are consequences to not following the process. Take for instance, the steps it takes to set up your business with the Secretary of State, the IRS, etc. If you bypass this part of the process, you will experience uncomfortable and unnecessary consequences; all of which could have been avoided.

We have to understand that the process will not kill us. It is there to help us grow. It is what will help us better understand what it takes to become an entrepreneur. It is what God uses to grow us, teach us, shape us, and mold us. Just as the not-so-pretty caterpillar must go through the process of becoming a beautiful butterfly, we must do so as well. Also like the caterpillar's transformation into a butterfly, if the process is interfered with, the transformation will be incomplete and what emerges will be half- complete or maybe even deformed.

4. Mistake:　　　Having an island mentality.

Solution:　　　Build a success circle.

Details:　　　I have heard entrepreneurs say, "it's easier to do it all myself." Six months, nine months or a year later, they are burned out and ready to quit. It's very easy to fall into the trap of thinking you can do it all alone. The reality is that every entrepreneur needs help. We may not all need the same kind of help, but we need help.

I have an entrepreneur who constantly pours into me much of the knowledge she has gained over the years. When I hear her speak about the early days where she had no one to help her, I understand how tough that was for her. I have come to understand the struggles and mistakes she made that were in part because she was a pioneer female entrepreneur. She intentionally poured into those who have come behind her to help us avoid some of the same traps.

Every entrepreneur is not able to receive this type of sound council. They will continue to move down a path that is dangerous and unproductive and then wonder why success escapes them.

The success circle is also important for support. I have someone in my success circle who listens to me. He listens to my good and my bad. He doesn't judge. He prays and then comes back with a word from the Lord or sound advice based on his life experiences.

I have learned to listen to those who have been where I'm trying to get to. The lessons I've learned and the support I've gained from my success circle have been invaluable.

5. Mistake: Copying, Mimicking and Stealing

   Solution: Be authentic.

Details: I see many entrepreneurs who research people in their industry which, if done properly, can be a good thing. It's great to learn from those who have gone before you. This can, in many cases, keep you from making many of the mistakes that other entrepreneurs have made. I have learned a great deal from studying and watching other entrepreneurs in my industry.

However, this approach becomes problematic when an entrepreneur attempts to copy or mimic the exact model of the individual they have studied. The model that works for one entrepreneur is unique to that individual. It won't necessarily fit any and everyone else. When you begin to copy, you can only copy the part you are able to see. What you can't see is the backroom moving parts of the model or system. This is the brains and heart of the model or system you're studying. This is what makes that particular entrepreneur successful. That cannot be duplicated because it's their why.

In my opinion, this also makes you look lazy. It makes it appear that you are too lazy to come up with your own model or system. It makes it appear that you lack the confidence, intelligence, and strength to create your own signature brand, products and systems. Inevitably, the entrepreneur will fail because they can only copy what they see. They can't copy the behind the scenes work that another entrepreneur is doing which is what makes them successful.

In conclusion, I have made many mistakes on my entrepreneurial journey. But what I also have tried to do is never make the same mistake multiple times. I have had many ups and downs as I've tried different paths to success. I have found that the solutions and suggestions I offer in this section will lead you to a level of success that you will find exciting.

I commend you on your willingness to take the entrepreneurial plunge. It is an exhilarating and sometimes frightening journey. The reward will in most cases far outweigh any frustrations you experience. Now, I will not tell you it is easy. If it were an easy journey, everyone would be a highly successful entrepreneur. What I will tell you is to continue to move forward with your calling and vision. Let hurdles be just that, hurdles. A hurdle is something you can jump over. Don't allow hurdles to become an insurmountable brick wall. You can go beyond where you are and get to where you want to be; to your *Place of Excellence™*.

Connect with Michelle Edelen!
Facebook: Always Excel
Twitter: @michelle_edelen
Periscope: @michelle_edelen
Email: michelle@excellenceinall.com
www.excellenceinall.com

Meet Mia D. Earl, Ph.D., Certified Wellness Coach who shares a holistic approach to assist individuals in achieving and maintaining optimal wellness that includes coaching, education, and reflexology that helps balance the systems of the body, as well as wellness products.

Power of God's Plan:
Path to Peace and Prosperity

"Many are the plans in the mind of a man, but it is the purpose of the Lord that will stand."

- Proverbs 19:21 (ESV)

As I reflect on my journey to becoming an entrepreneur, all I can say is that it was not my plan. I must share with you my story so that you may also appreciate the significance and gratitude of my five years as an entrepreneur. I must be clear, although there were twists and turns along my path, I have had a wonderful life. It was the blessings of prior years that stabilized me during my five years of entrepreneurship.

I did what most are told to do: Go to school, get a "good" job, and you will live a "good "life. Well, there is definitely more to life's journey than following those steps. However, I thought I was following the plan. I received my B.S., finished graduate school with a Master's in Public Health (MPH): Community Health Education, had completed an intern at the Veterans' Hospital in Little Rock, AR and expected to land a "good" job in my field of study.

I expected to marry the love of my life, my sweetheart, and live happily ever after. Therefore, I decided to reside in Memphis, TN where my fiancé at that time was located. Although not my dream job after college, I accepted the first job offered to me in Memphis. Little did I know that the plans I had for my life would be short lived. My fiancé decided to relocate to pursue a different career path which forced us into a long distance relationship.

Our plans to spend our lives together took a sudden turn as we both explored life and our relationship was jeopardized. With no expectation of ending our lives together, our path towards uniting came to a complete halt. Now left to deal with unintentional hurt, I found myself in a city I did not like without any close relatives, but I knew I must press forward. I decided to stay in Memphis. I told myself I would give this city five years and determine my next move.

On my career path, the first job lasted one year due to the stress that came along with it. I now believe God placed me there with the purpose of discovering an issue I had suppressed and was forced to deal with on this path called *life*. My experience with the first job took me to the second job with better pay and a management position within one year.

Again, this was not my field of choice, but provided valuable experience. This job experience helped prepare me for the path God had for me. A door was opened with another company for a part-time position in my field as a health educator which I enjoyed. But God had set me up … an opening then became available for a full-time position, and I was hired in the field of my choice. Again, within one year I was approached with the opportunity to be in a management role.

Then there were talks of the company closing its doors. It was at that moment that I knew I must have a plan B. With my passion for health and wellness and understanding the role that stress plays on the body, I started Abundant Life Wellness which provided stress management workshops with aromatherapy. As I faced the politics of management, I was determined that I would be true to my values and character. I pursued a job change that resulted in $10,000 less pay with the increased responsibility of project implementation.

Many thought I was out of my mind. At the time, I was seeking a peace of mind and not a salary. My Heavenly Father clearly showed me that provisions were made as I truly was not lacking anything with the decrease in salary. A door was later opened for another Project Director Position which increased my salary. God showed me again that with trust and obedience, provisions are made. However, I faced the challenges of corporate politics again. Management issues overtook the joy that came with helping others meet their health and wellness needs. I weathered the storm.

I began thinking long-term about my career path. God kept placing me in management positions. At this point, I had no desire to supervise people any longer. I wanted to do something with a hands-on approach. After several considerations with prayer and research, God laid out the path for his plan. I was introduced to reflexology. All I wanted was a good "foot rub". With continued encounters with reflexology, it was beneficial to my own health and healing.

However, it was a year or so later when I made the connection that I prayed for something hands on, and God placed reflexology in my path which intertwined with my health education background and experience. I researched schools, trained, and became certified as a reflexologist. I had no knowledge of where it would take me and at that time did not intend to pursue reflexology full time. I knew it was God's plan because all lined up with scheduling training and completing certifications.

I recall attending a women's conference with my church on a Friday night, getting home after 12:00 am and leaving at 4:00 am to drive by myself three and half hours to be in an 8:00 am reflexology class for the weekend. Nobody but God protected me. The training was not as easy as I thought. With the knowledge I had to gain to become certified, one would have thought I was in medical school. God made the path to reflexology obtainable.

After I completed my MPH program, I told myself I would never go back to school to obtain a degree. Well, God had another plan. God planted the seed to pursue my Ph.D. with a focus in Natural Health. I obtained that degree and my dissertation involved reflexology. It was the power of God's plan working in my life.

My vision was to one day work for myself to escape the harsh realities of corporate America. Well, that day came prematurely when the program I was managing at the time received word that it was phasing out and the positions would be eliminated. With a 30-day notice, I had little strength to seek another job. It was that day I made one of the best decisions of my life by officially launching my very own reflexology practice.

Lessons Learned/Pearls of Wisdom:

- **God is waiting on us to take action**. Follow God's path and God will show up. For about 6 months I rented a space to perform reflexology services. While visiting a sorority sister to support her business, she and I ended up having an extremely beneficial conversation. This led to God putting it on my heart to look into the vacant office spaces in that area. I trusted Him, cleared a savings account, and pursued the purchase of my own office space. With a made-up mind, I was determined I would no longer be in a position where I had to follow rules that I did not agree with and jeopardize my character. I would not put my values and integrity on the line. That was December 2010. I opened doors to a full-time wellness and reflexology practice January 2011, *Abundant Life Wellness Solutions.*

- **Follow your Dreams.** Others may not see the vision God has planted within you, but you must be careful not to live for their approval. Be faithful and follow what God has put in your heart. I had a desire to own my office space and not rent. Therefore, I had to seek options that were affordable for me at that time.

  I asked a friend to visit office locations with me and give me feedback on the location. This friend was not positive and made me feel that I should not pursue ownership of office space.

  I remember asking someone I knew with a cleaning service to provide me with a quote of what it would cost to clean the building. After viewing the space, she stated that it appeared the area was changing, and it may not be the best location for me. I talked with the acupuncturist and a salon owner who had been in the area since it was developed. I noticed a thriving cardiologist across from my building. God showed me this space and I had to trust Him. I did not wait for their approval, placed a couple of offers for the office space and it was accepted.

  If I had listened to others who did not see my vision for this office space and had not trusted God's plan for this space, I may not have pursued my dream of office ownership.

- **God will give us exactly what we need when we need it.** We must trust and believe. Now that I had the office space, I had to build my clientele. I remembered a contact with a well know company in the area and scheduled a meeting with them. I submitted a proposal and received approval to offer my reflexology services. This was my confirmation that I was walking in direct alignment to God's path. I believe strongly that if God can open this door, surely others will be opened as well.

- **God will supply all of my needs**. I later entered into another relationship, got married, and took my vows seriously. God showed me this marriage was not the plan for my life. I ended up divorced, left with traumatic, separating issues and had to deal with the shame and guilt of domestic violence. While on my path to peace and prosperity, I went from two incomes to one income, unemployment to self-employment and all was taken care of. I was placed in a position to totally depend on the promises of God. The scripture that tells me Christ will never leave nor forsake me has become a true testament in my life.

- **Be Persistent**. Although I faced the aftermath of a divorce and the loss of a job, I did not allow it to keep me from my purpose – to serve others. The pressure and pain of life propelled my plan of entrepreneurship. Whatever challenges I faced, whatever circumstances weighted me down, I made a choice to remain persistent and refuse to be distracted.

In January 2016, I celebrated five years of entrepreneurship with a reflexology and wellness practice in Memphis, TN. If you understand the dynamics of reflexology and wellness in a place such as Memphis, TN, you will know that it was not an easy path to travel. When I look at where God has brought me from on this career path of over 20 years and the challenges I faced, I am filled with tears of gratitude. There were life's storms that I did not see my way out of, but God intervened right on time. God protected and provided for me every step of the way.

I have a reflexology practice of clients that appreciate my services and help me to be grateful for the gift of my hands. I have peace and am fulfilled with the joy of seeing my clients free from pain and reaping the benefits of reflexology and improved wellness. I am able to create an environment of peace for others. I have met wonderful individuals whom God placed in my path to unconditionally assist me along this journey.

With all of my years of education, I never thought my peace and prosperity would come from a hands-on approach of touching feet. (ha!) My passion and sincerity shows in what I do. I am asked frequently, *"How do you touch other's feet?"* Or *"Do you really enjoy what you do?"* I continue to trust God in where he leads me on this journey of life and entrepreneurship.

While in pursuit of my destiny which led me to entrepreneurship, I've witnessed others make the following mistakes:

No industry experience – Something may have been a hobby, but the person has never worked in the industry. A solution is to find a mentor in that industry and become engaged in what it takes to survive.

Insufficient startup capital – The person has elaborate plans and dreams but does not have the capital to sustain the start-up. A solution is to develop a sensible budget with potential income and expenses. Seek out loan options and an advisor.

1. **Lack of accounting or business knowledge** – The person is great in their profession but does not have the skills needed to maintain the bookkeeping. A solution is to partner with someone who has accounting and business experiences. If budget permits, hire a bookkeeper or an accountant.

2. **Wrong location** – The service or product does not meet the need of where the business is located. A solution is to look at the service or product being offered and seek a location in which there is a demand.

3. **Failure to pay taxes as required** – Some people do not understand the tax requirements or make the choice not to pay taxes based on lack of income to support the business. Prioritize the payment of taxes and seek counsel as needed.

In addition to witnessing the mistakes of others, I myself have also made quite a few mistakes of my own. They are:

1. **Having a desire to help "everyone"**- I wanted others to improve their health or circumstances more than they wanted it. I "gave away" services and attempted to convince others that they needed what I had to offer. I shifted my mindset. The services I offered were not for everyone. Those that valued my services would pay for it. My task is to educate others on what I have to offer and allow them to make an informed decision.

2. **Trying to do it all alone**- I had to utilize the expertise of others and trust others with bookkeeping.

3. **Ineffective Communication**– I had to speak facts and leave out personal emotions when it comes to business.

4. **Fear of failure** – I had to trust my Heavenly Father. I saw myself as a servant and created an environment of caring and quality services.

5. **Failing to Follow-up** - Keep in touch with clients/customers. It is okay to ask for business, schedule next appointment, and ask for referrals.

6. **Lack of solid relationships** - It is okay to know a lot of people but dedicate time to building and nurturing those relationships. Don't just know people to know them but remain close to those who will uplift, inspire, and motivate you to be all you were created to be. Know that you have something to offer others and they have something to offer you as well.

7. **Inconsistency in your banding message-** Build a brand of trust and respect. Be dependable. As an entrepreneur it is my desire and mission to build a brand in which I am seen as the "go to person", an expert in my field.

I am grateful for everything that happened in my life because I believe it was God's plan to mold me into the person I am today and give me the strength to endure the path of entrepreneurship. It is God's purpose and path for my life to bring hope and healing through reflexology and other natural health modalities!

I challenge you to make the decision to pursue entrepreneurship if it is truly in your spirit and it is God's path for you. It is not what happens to you or what you have or don' have that is important, it is the mindset and the decisions that you make to follow the path God leads you on.

"Trust in the Lord with all your heart, and do not lean on your own understanding. In all your ways acknowledge him, and he will make straight your path." (Proverbs 3:5-6 ESV)

Connect with Mia Earl via Facebook at:
Abundant Life Well
www.abundantlifewellness-solutions.com

Meet Cheryl Holland, Brand strategist & Professional Coach who is committed to empowering female entrepreneurs on how to build an exceptional, empowerment brand, accumulate more clients while making money online without compromising her integrity.

Developing My Conduit for Blessing

I believe we should have our cake & eat it too. That means to do what you love and get paid well for it. I believe that God has given each and every one of us a purpose to fulfill and that we fulfill that purpose using the gifts and talents that He's blessed us with. I call it the 'The Conduit for Blessing™". If we want the blessing of wealth so that we can truly be a blessing to others, then we need to have a conduit to receive the wealth. It will not come through a job. I believe it only comes by creating your own value through entrepreneurship.

So, I took a leap without a net. I didn't have a financial net and I certainly didn't have a proper faith net at the time. And guess what happened? I crashed and burned.

This was in 2003 when I made my first attempt at entrepreneurship. The company I'd worked for was going through a reorganization and after being there 18 years, I was faced with a decision. Do I stay or do I leave?

You see, all employees in my department had to reapply for their jobs. I was blessed in that I was offered a position in a different department doing my same job and making the same money. I was making $56,000 a year and (along with my husband's income) so we were doing pretty well.

But I wanted more. I knew I was meant for more. Not more money necessarily, but I knew that I was called for more than working for 30 plus years at the same company that I'd started working for the Monday after graduating high school. While most would've been satisfied with the 'security' of that scenario, I just couldn't imagine that being my life.

So, I turned down the job offer, and you'd think that I had just committed a first degree felony based on the reaction that followed.

The hiring manager basically told me that I was crazy. He could not understand how, when so many were losing their jobs, I could just give mine up. I told him that I planned to start my own graphic and web design company and he looked at me like I had two heads. What happened next floored me!

He called my boss, the Vice President of Human Resources, while he was on vacation in Arizona with his family and told him to call me and talk some sense into me. And my boss actually called me on his vacation. I told him the same thing about starting my own company and that he wouldn't be able to change my mind. So, he resigned to the fact that there wasn't a thing he could do about it.

I began my official journey to entrepreneurship. I filed the DBA (doing business as) for A'Sista Design & Publishing. I created my website. I told a limited number of people about my business and then I...waited. Thinking about it now it's kind of funny, but I really believed at the time that if I build it (my business and website) they will come. I didn't know a thing about getting traffic, I just knew how to design websites.

As you can probably guess…I had no clients and wasn't making any money. I was collecting unemployment and it was approaching the time to report what jobs I had applied for so I could continue to receive funds. Well, I hadn't applied for any. So, because I wasn't making money in my business and wanted to continue to get unemployment, I searched and applied for two jobs. Within a week I had interviews scheduled for both and then offered and accepted one of the positions.

Just like that my full-time entrepreneurial endeavor was over; however, I did get some small jobs through referrals on a part-time basis.

Parallel to this time I was following my call and passion to empower women. I hosted women's workshops at my church called Ministry, Marriage & Motherhood. I also formed the A'Sista Accountability Group and met women in my home to empower them to plan and achieve their goals. I had no idea that I was coaching back then. I was coaching before it was called coaching. I also didn't realize that the Lord was preparing me for the path He designed for me related to entrepreneurship. You'll understand soon how this all ties together, just stick with me here.

I loved working with women and encouraging them to embrace the power within them to achieve great things. I loved hosting women's ministry events at my church…but unfortunately that came to an ugly and screeching halt and caused me to put my dream on hold for about five years. What happened was that one of the women in my church who had worked on my team for our workshops left the church to pastor with her husband. It was fine, no hard feelings were involved in her departure at all. What happened shortly after was the issue.

She decided to take the workshop format that I created and conduct her own. Now I really wouldn't have had a problem with that if she decided to incorporate it in her new church. Why re-invent the wheel? However, I would have appreciated it if she'd discussed it with me since it was my baby. But she didn't and that's not even the real issue. The problem came in when she decided that she wanted to host her workshop (which was my workshop with a new name) at our church.

This sister approached our pastor who then presented it to me and the team of ladies working on our workshop. I was flabbergasted at the nerve of her to do this! My pastor convinced us to support it by saying that we would not have to do any of the work, simply help pass out her flyers and support by attending. So, we agreed.

Well, low and behold, the next week we were told that we need to make copies of the flyers. Then we were told to let her use our supplies. We had purchased materials for our workshops such as notebooks, bags, pens, gifts, favors, etc. But here's the kicker. We purchased all of that from money out of our own pockets. We did not use the church funds for this. So, I objected to giving her our supplies, especially since we had our next workshop that we were planning coming up soon. It went downhill from there.

That evening, my pastor called me and said that she decided that we are canceling our women's workshop. It was an emotional decision on her part because of my objection. I was hurt and disappointed. I decided that I would not do another one EVER!

The Lord had a different plan though. Years later the desire and ideas for workshops continued to flood my mind and heart. I'd since left my previous church. Not because of the workshop incident by the way. I'd stayed years after that and left on great terms. I don't believe in leaving a church because of an offense. I stay where I'm led until God releases me. But I was in another church where I knew that I could potentially be in a position of the workshops being "controlled" in a sense. I knew what the Lord had given me, and I did not want to have to conform to something that was not in line with his plan for my life in relation to my vision. So, I sat on my dream a little longer.

Fast forward a few years later. My assignment at that church was completed. While I was attending the church I would later join, I was also planning my first Permission Granted Women's Empowerment Seminar. This was in 2011. I knew that I was called to empower women outside of the church walls. Some of the women that I needed to reach would not come if I hosted the event in a church building. Therefore, I held it at a local hotel, and it was very successful in the sense that I had a great turn out. That was all that was important to me at the time. I wasn't thinking about this as business. This was my purpose and passion. It was my call. My only focus was empowering women. I didn't realize at the time that there was more to it.

Back in 2007, while I was still working full-time, I began to get that entrepreneur itch again. I decided to scratch it by revamping. I formed A'Sista Media Group, LLC and began to intentionally grow my business with the hopes of being able to do it full-time. Every year I became more and more anxious to leave my job. I was starting to dislike it. I was going in later and later because I was literally dragging myself out of bed and forcing myself to show up there. I hated it. Not the work. Not the people. What I hated was simply being there because I wanted to work on and in my business. I wanted to travel, speak, and empower women. So, during my 9 to 5, I could barely do the job they were paying me to do because my focus was totally on my dream. I knew that I had to take that leap again.

And then it clicked with the help of my pastor. On one Sunday morning during his message, he said something that changed my entire perspective and opened my mind up to a whole new aspect of what God had for me. My pastor, Rodney R. Roberts, said *"Your prosperity is tied to your purpose."* That's when it hit me.

I had tried to have two different avenues of focus. My branding business and then my purpose of empowering women was separate. As a matter of fact, I had two different websites. It was not effective because I had two different visions which is division. A divided vision, even if it's just within you, cannot stand for the long term.

Now I can see that these two areas were meant to be intricately connected. Empowering women is my business. It so happens that I not only empower them spiritually and emotionally but also in business. Those three are also intricately connected as well.

My challenge then was, how can I do this without compromising my integrity? Because for me, empowering women had been ministry in a sense. It wasn't about the money, and I didn't want it to ever be about the money. I eventually realized that my block about money was, in part, one of the reasons I was stuck in my business. I had to become okay with making money, and lots of it, doing something I absolutely loved. But it was this final straw that pushed me over the edge.

My former superintendent came into my office flashing a big goofy grin and handed me an envelope and his hand to shake. He thanked me for my service for the last year and said how great a job I was doing.

I knew the envelope held my annual merit increase letter because I'd gone through this same song and dance (with different partners) over the 10 years I'd worked there. The letter said that my raise was $1527 for the year. But this time after opening and reading that letter, something was different. I wasn't smiling. I wasn't excited. I WAS DISGUSTED! I knew that I could make that in one day in my own business. I couldn't handle working for someone else anymore. I had to go.

But this time my leap into entrepreneurship had to be different because I had no intention in ever having to work for someone else again. So, because I wanted it to be different, I knew I had to do something different. I hired a business coach. I knew that I needed help if I was going to make it happen. After all, I'd

Googled information, downloaded free e-books, and attended free workshops and classes. Those were helpful but I was still missing some critical pieces to this business puzzle that left me making a minimal income from my business. I had to invest in my dream. I had to get out of my comfort zone and make something happen.

When I made my first $10,000 a month in income, I was convinced about this entrepreneur life. It's God plan to make a difference in the world and to create a conduit of blessing for ourselves because "prosperity is tied to our purpose." So now, I help other empowering women entrepreneurs to reach their first $10k month.

I'm having my cake & eating it to and I'm loving what I do!

However, in the midst of all of my success along my entrepreneurial journey I have made a few mistakes and have listed them below:

1. **Poor Money Mindset:** When I first started out, I was focused on FREE. If it was free, then it was for me. If I could Google it to find an answer, I was good. Or so I thought. What I later realized is that my actions were a result of a poor money mindset and was keeping me broke. In my mind I couldn't afford anything that wasn't free. What I later realized is that I was working against the law of reciprocity and trying to reap where I hadn't sown. How could I expect someone to invest money with me as a coach, if I wasn't willing to do the same? So, I hired a business coach although I had no idea where the money was going to come from. I still can't explain exactly how I got the money, but what I can tell you is that the money came and in turn I began to get clients that paid me. Money likes action and movement. You must invest in your dream.

2. **Afraid of Marketing:** Marketing was one of the hardest things for me to do starting out. My understanding of marketing at the time took me way out of my comfort zone.

I hated selling. So, the thought of marketing just made me shrink back. However, I knew that if I wanted my business to succeed, I would have to just get over it. I found a way to do that by understanding what I offer is truly transformational for the women I serve. It would be horrible for me to have the answer they're looking for and never tell them about it. So, when you can think of marketing as "serving" instead of "selling", it makes all of the difference. At least it did for me. If you can solve your clients' problem, be bold about telling them about what you offer. It doesn't have to be salesy. It's a matter of identifying the problem and communicating the value in your solution to solve that problem.

3. **Perfectionism.** That "p" word leads to another one...procrastination. I was gripped by both and what I discovered was that it was rooted in fear. The same root cause that led me to shrink back with my marketing. The truth of the matter is that perfection in business not realistic. The more you procrastinate trying to reach perfection, the less people you serve, the less lives you help transform and the less money you make to create the abundant life you desire and was promised.

4. **Following the Wrong Business Model:** When I first transitioned my business from graphic and web design to include brand coaching, I struggled with a marketing sales funnel that not only fit my income needs but that fit my personality as well. I connected with my coach on so many levels and had great success with her. What I later discovered is that I couldn't follow her business model long term. It was draining for me and so outside of my personality. I needed a more streamlined approach. I adapted what I learned from her and combined it with other strategies that better fit me and created a $10k/ month strategies that was less stressful and suited for the introvert in me. My suggestion is to get clear on what business model

will work for the lifestyle you desire to create. How many days a week do you want to work? How many hours? Do you enjoy networking? Do you want to travel? Be sure that you learn a process that fits your business income and lifestyle goals.

5. **Trying to do everything myself:** I am a multi-talented 'recovering' do-it-yourselfer, and it almost killed my business. Because I was never one to ask for help with anything, I took that same attitude into my business. This caused me to be overwhelmed and lose potential clients through the cracks. I spent way too much time in the beginning on tasks that should have been delegated. I learned the hard way, but I finally did get the message and secured an assistant to help me run my business. I learned to let go. I listed everything I was doing in my business and for each task I determined which ones I needed to handle and the others I placed in the hands of my assistant. Accepting and recognizing the need for help is a must.

Here are the mistakes I have witnessed other entrepreneurs make:

1. **Launching without a profit plan.** This is especially true for women's empowerment entrepreneurs whose main focus is to empower women and want to do it full-time. They are full of passion and ideas, but typically do not have clarity on *how* to actually make money with those ideas. Especially if her desire is to empower women full-time. To be successful you have to know your numbers. Start with how much money you desire to make per month. What is the cost of your service/product? How many clients need to purchase your products in order for you to meet your money goal? How do you plan to make that happen? Answer those questions and you have a basic plan to get started and at least know what your goal is.

2. **Undercharging**. This is one of the most frustrating mistakes new entrepreneurs make. You know you want and need to make money, but you're afraid to charge what you desire because you don't think people will pay it. One of the best lessons I learned was to "stay out of people's pockets". In other words, stop assuming people don't have money to pay the price you really want and deserve. People pay for what they value. PERIOD. As long as you can fully express the value you bring to the table, charge what your services are truly worth. One of the exercises I give my coaching clients when figuring out pricing is to have them list ALL of the benefits and outcomes for the client if they make a purchase. This allows them to begin to see the true value of what they're providing and the confidence to increase prices.

3. **Not Clearly Identifying Your Ideal Client.** When first starting a business, you want clients. Any clients, as long as they're paying clients. The new entrepreneur focuses and markets to everyone. The problem one runs into with this mindset is that everyone does not want or need your service or product. And, unless you have an extremely large marketing budget, you cannot effectively market to everyone. It's extremely important for new entrepreneurs, especially when growing your business online, to narrow your target audience because when you're speaking to everyone, you're actually speaking to no one, and you get lost in the online marketplace. You may be on social media and people "like" your stuff, but they won't necessarily "buy" your stuff. Why? Because your message isn't speaking directly to a problem that they want solved. Clearly identify who you best serve and get to know them intimately.

4. **Expecting Family Support.** I hear this complaint all the time. New entrepreneurs feeling let down and betrayed by family and friends who don't support their business. My

response: Get over it! That's just the way it is. The bottom line is that you don't know enough about being an entrepreneur yet if this is bothering you. Separate your business from your interpersonal emotions. An entrepreneur is successful because he or she has a product or service that solves a problem for a specific audience, not because your family bought your stuff. Unless your family or friends are your target audience, why are you pressing them to buy from you? You have the wrong focus. And even if they are an ideal client, you must express the value of what you offer to them, just like you do any other potential client.

5. **Focusing on the Visual Brand First.** Your visual brand is your logo, website, and colors. So many new entrepreneurs jump right in and spend money on these pieces up front without having developed an actual brand strategy. When this happens, many times there will be a disconnect between your visual brand and your audience. Your visual brand should not be considered until you, at a minimum, know who your ideal clients is, what problem you solve for him/her, what your standout message is to attract him/her and what values you want to present to that audience. If not, you could be wasting time and money.

Connect with Cheryl Holland today!
Twitter/Facebook/Instagram:@asistaproject
www.asistaproject.com

Meet Cassandra B. Elliott, native of Brooklyn, New York, vocal and empowerment coach who offers various trainings and serves locally as an Assistant Pastor. For 12 years she lived with kidney disease, then battled breast cancer seven years later. In both cases, she received supernatural healing by trusting in God and has been given a clean bill of health as of July 2014. Below she shares her story that is sure to empower, encourage and uplift you to operate in your divine calling un-apologetically.

DISCLAIMER: Since the publishing of this book, Pastor Cassandra B. Elliott has passed away, and what you are reading is apart of her legacy.

Purpose Revealed in the Midst of Pain

"Being confident in this, that he who began a good work in you will carry it on to completion until the day of Christ Jesus."- Philippians 1:6

I am a native New Yorker and I have been a leader since childhood. I showed leadership academically and creatively at an early age. I was definitely a leader in my church. I started playing the piano at 6 years of age. I played the piano at my elementary graduation which was a highlight for me and my family. I graduated from the famous "Fame" high school, brought to life on the big screen. There my leadership abilities began to blossom even the more. I was a freshman but functioning like a senior because of the access that was given to me! I really believe here is where my purpose was activated.

I didn't have all of the details, but I felt a great pull towards helping people walk into their purpose. I had wisdom beyond my years. At this time, I was introduced to mentoring in my high school years. Someone took me under their wing and made sure I walked along the right path. It was a great time of accountability that had a tremendous effect on my life. To this day we are still connected.

Years after, people were drawn to me because of the wisdom I possessed. My phone rang continually. I was always called upon to give natural and spiritual wisdom. I received calls from all over the United States. I naturally fell into purpose! As I traveled the country, I connected with so many people. I helped with internal issues with individuals as well corporate systemic issues. I was a trusted voice and was called upon continually and that was a tremendous blessing.

Even in my time of sickness, God allowed me to be able to continue to serve. I am so grateful. My calling and purpose didn't change because of my physical affliction. Actually, things shifted dramatically. I was able to hear more clearly, and the connections and calls began to increase. I was able to walk out my purpose in the midst of the pain. No matter what I continued to encourage others during this trying time. My life spoke to the people I mentored to push them into purpose despite delays and detours!

In the year of 2002, an opportunity opened for me and my husband. Although I was still suffering with renal failure we moved to North Carolina. I knew there was purpose for us moving to the south. Soon it was revealed why. This is where I began coaching more worship leaders (and overall leaders as well.) I was able to sit with them and share pearls of wisdom to help further equip them for their ministry. I held them to a high standard of accountability. This was required!

Soon after, Pastors and churches asked me to come in and train their music ministry. They wanted to ensure the leaders in this area were properly equipped not only in music but in skill as well as character. Mentoring and coaching to me is life giving. Seeing the result of my time with individuals I pour into is invaluable. I love celebrating their successes but also being there to encourage them in times of failures and weakness.

From the mentorship I have released two signature programs. The first is "5 Essential Tools that Every Worship Leader Needs" and the second is "No Excuses!" The first program is for individuals that serve in the arena of music and the second programs is for others who desire to stop giving power to their excuses and live out their life's purpose in the earth.

I have seen growth and maturity in all those I coach. They have made an investment in themselves which tells me they care about adding value to their life. I am so grateful for this ability to be a conduit in the lives of those that are at a crossroad. They choose me to direct them, establish the roadmap, and help them navigate to their desired destination and result.

My Story Continues...

I will never forget that day. I was at the altar ministering to the youth and one of my ministry team members came over to me. He said, *"God wants me to share this word with you."* I stood still and prepared myself to hear what God would say to me. He said *"God says do what I told you to do. Stop being concerned about what everyone else is doing and do what I said to do."* I knew it was God speaking directly to me.

God and I were having this conversation and I learned I was making excuses! I literally said God why should I do that and everyone else is doing it? At that point I had to put that excuse away. It was not working for God! In less than 30 days from when He reminded me and reprimanded, I moved in what I knew to do. I birthed what I saw in my prayer time. Everything fell into place. Announcement to singers, minstrels, liturgical dance, location, ministry team, out of town guests, to finances! It was an amazing night of Kingdom ministry.

I literally could feel the weight of the vision and God's approval. The room was filled with expectation. Three years later after a successful kidney transplant, I was standing in the moment of my healing, victory, and manifested obedience! My words seem so inadequate! I wish I could take you back to that moment when I stood on the stage, and I could see what all the suffering and affliction was about. God had literally authenticated the anointing on my life. He could trust that I would worship in that moment and give Him all the glory.

My obedience propelled me into what I now see nine years later. I could have let my excuses build a wall between me and my purpose, and obedience. I am so grateful that I heard an obeyed.

As it relates to my own entrepreneurial journey, I have made a few mistakes and have listed them below:

1. **Not Having the Right Team**

   a. There are times when you feel because you know people and their abilities, that they are the right fit. This was not a positive move for me. I was very disappointed in their performance because of familiarity.

   b. Choose people that are skilled and qualified that understand their roles. They are personable but put their job and work above relationship in order to ensure your success.

2. **Poor Time Management**

a. Poor time management was a mistake for me as well. I am very self-reliant, but ministry and travel made my life full. After a while I saw that important business matters were not being handled in excellence.

b. I had to ask for help. When I realized I was not functioning in excellence I had to find an administrative team. The team handles different aspects of your business. It lets you be the visionary and trust the team to carry out the details of your vision

3. Getting Discouraged

a. You must believe in what you are called to build. You were created to release in the earth what you were created to do

b. Make sure you have a group of people that can encourage you to keep building. They are there to be truthful with you in your areas of short coming as well as give wise counsel concerning your life and business.

4. Making Excuses

a. There were times in my life that I talked myself out of my purpose because I didn't feel like I had all I needed to be as great as others

b. It is important to have purpose partners in your life that know your heart and your vision. They check in with you to remind you of who you are and what you are capable of accomplishing.

5. Team Changes

a. Finally, one of the hardest things I dealt with was becoming emotional in reference to team changes.

There will be times when your team must be upgraded. Even when there are those who were with you from the beginning, you must be open to them walking away. I was so distraught, even angry and felt abandoned. I even felt betrayed.

b. You must step back and assess your emotions. After prayer and really listening to God, I had to realize that it wasn't about me, but they were in another season of their life. I should have been grateful for their service. After understanding this, I was able to wish them well and remain in relationship with them. For this I am grateful!!!

Here are the mistakes I have witnessed other entrepreneurs make:

1. Failing to Establish a WINNING Team

a. When you do not have the right team, there will be unproductive times in business. You spend too much time trying to be business owner and coach.

b. The solution is to make sure there are clear objectives for each team members' position. Allow them to function with measurable goals and clear communication.

2. Lack of Proper Time Management

a. You must manage your time to be successful. In business you represent yourself and your brand.

b. The solution to this is enlisting the right tools and the right systems. An administrative assistant is a great tool. Your administrator makes you look good and helps keep you on track so that you and your brand can be trusted to serve in excellence

3. Unclear Vision

a. When there is an unclear vision, those that work with you will produce what they think you want, and not produce what you need.

b. It is important that your vision for the business is in written form and reviewed on consistent bases, especially when changes occur.

4. Poor Money Matters

a. I have seen businesses spend money and have no account for their output.

b. It is important to have a proper accountant that can help you see your expenditures as well as your profit. This builds a reputable business that can attract investors as well as business partners.

5. Mixing Friendships with Business

a. This can bè a recipe for disaster. Friendship and business if not handled properly, can destroy both leaving lives in shambles.

b. The solution is that both parties must be very open and truthful about the parts they play. Putting the partnership in writing is for the safety of both parties. If there is ever a crossing of boundaries that have been set, a restructuring or dissolving of partnership may be necessary in order to keep the friendship intact. It really depends on where they value lies: The Business or the friendship.

Connect with Cassandra Today!
Twitter: @PC_Elliott
Facebook: Cassandra Elliott
Instagram: @pcelliott
www.cassandraelliott.com

Meet Cierra Michelle, Founder of Single Mothers for Christ who is committed to the advancement of others. She is also a professional coach who offers a developmental program for women in an effort to encourage and provide them with the necessary tools and resources needed to live extraordinary lives through Jesus Christ.

Don't Allow Your Past to Intimidate Your Future

As a high-school dropout and a repeated sexual abuse victim, my mind, was constantly consumed with thoughts of self-infliction. I felt as if I didn't have anything to offer the world; let alone myself. I grew up having a very tumultuous relationship with my mother, which included years of verbal abuse. Out of rebellion, I turned to a secret life of sex, drugs, and alcohol. Hearing that I would never be good enough for anything but lying on my back started to resonate with me. To numb the pain, I was turned to the streets and allowed men to have their way with my body. After being raped and molested from the age of 13-15 by my stepbrother and later a family friend, I could no longer identify any other way to feel beautiful except at the expense of other men's physical pleasure. I had officially checked out and became the ugly duckling to myself. I was numb.

While the rest of my peers were preparing to enter college and securing internships making names for themselves along the corporate ladder, I on the other hand worked low-end jobs making $4.75/hr and skipping my adult education class where I was scheduled to earn my GED to hang out at local motels with my "friends"

After several months of not being able to secure a stable job and getting fired from yet another one I applied to work at a local department store. Weeks later, I interviewed and was hired for a position at the jewelry counter. During breaks, I became infatuated and often glanced around the Health & Beauty department. I was very much intrigued by the beautiful array of cosmetic brands. Earlier on, I had taken an interest in cosmetics. I would buy makeup in bulk with the little money I had and spent hours practicing in the mirror on myself as well as my friends.

The store manager later offered me a promotion as the Health and Beauty Department Lead Manager with a considerable raise. She was very impressed with my customer service and makeup technique application. I was ecstatic! Months earlier, I sat under the tutelage of my older cousins at her local hair salon where they taught the basics of makeup application and personal style. This wasn't just a dream anymore; it was becoming my reality and I knew I wanted to be a makeup artist.

Months went by and with the new pay increase, I finally earned enough money to create and mold my own personal makeup kit. Gone were the days that I could only afford the dollar store brands. Soon after, I purchased my first pair of brushes. During this time, I had also taken a part-time entrepreneurial position as a Beauty Advisor for a direct selling company. I began networking exclusively at a variety of local hair salons and neighborhoods and was invited to host beauty parties for makeup application and services. I had limited access to the internet and was always on the go so my only direct avenues of marketing became my Alltel flip phone, catalogs provided by the manufacturer and word of mouth. I had literally become a walking billboard for branding and flourishing a lucrative career as a makeup artist.

Where pride and greed linger, so shall karma. I was making money, but I wanted more. I soon began shoplifting from my very own department in order to retain more money while I was making sales as a part time beauty coach. I diminished everything I worked so hard for and that summer I was fired from the department store. It was after this time; I went back into a deep depression and couldn't consistently meet my quotas under my direct selling commission. I received a letter days later announcing I was being dropped from the company. In less than a year, I was unemployed, with an overdrawn bank account and a now tarnished reputation. I had officially hit rock bottom…. again.

I later applied for a direct hire job at a call center and began to rationalize my purpose. In order for me to maintain a steady job, I would have to do something that provided me with longevity and most importantly security. I contacted a United States Army recruiter and considered taking the ASVAB (Armed Services Vocational Aptitude Battery.) After just two weeks, I convinced my mother to sign the contract allowing me to enlist and by March 2008, I was headed to boot camp. After I completed the training, I moved into my own apartment.

One evening, I came home to find an eviction notice giving me less than 30 days to have my belongings vacated. Here I was once again at rock bottom and had spent every dime of my bonus helping my mother and spending excessively on my shopping habits and friends. I packed up everything I could manage to keep in a green 32-gallon bucket and with the help of some friends moved out of my apartment in less than 24 hours. The next day, I was on my way to Washington, DC to transfer to another duty station. With my part time reservist pay, I would rent different motels just to have somewhere to sleep until a Master Sergeant I worked for offered me a room at no cost. Months later, I was offered a temporary position in Human Resources and later became a permanent federal employee.

The Sergeant First Class who hired me sat me down one day and had a heart to heart with me. She also began to question my work ethic and tardiness. I told her the only place I was fortunate to live was at least two hours away using public transportation. She offered me a room at minimal cost and gave me access to drive one of her cars to work. Here was my opportunity to make a change and turn my life around.

Weeks later, I found my way back into cosmetics and started applying for more and more jobs at local makeup counters around the city. Here I was a 19-year-old girl in the heart of Washington, DC with a passion to do makeup and make others feel beautiful. I had no idea how I would be able to pursue my dream, but I was determined to take back everything I lost years prior. I desired to be more than the girl with the tarnished reputation and a lack of moral standards. I was determined to take back those nights where I wrote in my diary how bad I wanted to die and would rather suffer my last breath than to be told once again that I should have been aborted and never given the opportunity to see the morning sun. I was determined to return from the ashes and capture the beautiful woman God had purposed me to be.

Fast-forward eleven years later, I am now the CEO and Creative Director of three businesses one of them being my passion. *Cierra Michelle Beauty (*a traveling Beauty Enterprise specializing in natural make-up application, skincare consulting and hosting beauty events), *Single Mothers For Christ* (a non-profit organization dedicated to helping single mothers capture the tools within themselves to propel into their God Destined purpose through the Gospel of Jesus Christ.) Lastly, my personal brand, *Cierra Michelle Speaks*, recently established as a developmental and faith based coaching program to encourage teenage women with unlikely backgrounds that getting to Jesus and living a life with Him is still possible. I aim to save the souls of those who counted themselves out.

Everything was against me and for a while I was even against me. I would look at my friends and be so full of discontent about life. How could they possibly be so happy while I felt as if I was a public spectacle? I felt incapable of returning from what was of my life and turning it into an atrium of endless and beautiful everlasting possibilities.

I was more than what I had gone through. Through all I had been through, I had to stand still and allow myself to be used by God not by the world.

Becoming an entrepreneur, I made several key mistakes and one was allowing the world to have input over my God led destiny. I didn't have a lot of money. I used only what I had until I was in a place of obtaining more. I wasn't popular and to this day I don't have tons and tons of notoriety. Does this alone make me not good enough? No! Does that make me less successful? Absolutely not! The world is who counted me out initially so why should I depend on the world to define what my worth looks like?

As an entrepreneur you have to use what was meant to destroy you and turn it into something that will propel and prepare you for the next level of your purpose. There were many times where my past could have allotted me the chance to give up, but I remained encouraged and pressed through. Your beginnings may appear small but have no underlying designation into the prosperity and how fast God can and will enlarge your territory. He sees each and every tear you've cried. (Psalms 56:8-9) God sees the moments when you've felt overlooked and undervalued. He sees you trying to plan events, and no one has shown up. Gods sees your faith. It could have been so easy for me to pray for God to give me a way out but then he wouldn't be doing me due diligence if every time I went through something he just removed it. Being broken isn't a bad thing and can be measured at different instances. It's like the broken glass effect. You take a glass and slam it on the floor, and you pick up the pieces. You try and find the exact pieces to repair this glass and although you've done a pretty decent job at finding some of the core pieces to repairing this glass, unbeknownst to you, there are still those small, tiny fragments that are missing. Which means, you no longer have 100% of the glass and may never be able to put the glass together the same way you found it. Does it mean you're permanently broken? Nope! Some of those tiny fragments although small in nature aided the big fragments in maintaining a smooth surface for the glass to appear ok.

As people and things hurt us, depending on the level of hurt, they begin to pick apart tiny fragments and those tiny particles make larger holes therefore, after you have found the larger pieces and you attempt to put your glass back together the glass really never returns to its original form because those tiny itty-bitty fragments were never replaced, found, or were swept away. You can only focus on the pieces you made it out with. You will confuse yourself if you bring an intimidated past into a pre-destined future. Use it to catapult you into your purpose. You don't see sports players resigning after they had a couple of rough games. But they create game plans, watch the footage, and get back in the game.

Being an entrepreneur in a busy and crowded marketplace can be discouraging and a tad overwhelming but it is also a matter of going from faith to faith.

Mistakes I Made as an Entrepreneur

- **Never stop investing in yourself and your brand.** For the longest time I wanted a thriving website to propel web business but didn't want to pay the beautiful website money.

- **Giving up before I started.** When I first started *Single Mothers for Christ*, my daughter had just turned one I didn't have a support system or any friends or family that believed in my dream. It was just the Holy Spirit and me. I didn't know how I was going to eat let alone run and manage a non-profit organization. Once I looked at the lack of revenue, I quickly wanted to give up without looking at the bigger picture

- **Making money the only motive.** If money is the only agenda, you might as well sign on to have a get rich quick scheme and not be an entrepreneur. Strive to make a difference and give your audience something they can use. More importantly, leave a valuable impression. Some of the best things are free. In a crowded entrepreneurial environment, people must know they can trust you and they certainly will not invest their money into to something or someone they wouldn't trust. Would you?

- **Glamorizing your business; wanting notoriety more than you want to help others.** Sure, having our names in lights is great and becoming well known has its privileges but what's a title if you don't even have the morale character to build a suitable clientele or audience? It's not about how many followers and "likes" you receive but more so about *why* they follow you. In other words, what makes you stand out?

- **Comparing your business to another.** No matter where you are in your business, someone else's increase is not your decrease. Don't measure your growth by someone else's growth. Focus on why you started and not where you are.

- **Not being comfortable with your voice.** This was a big one for me. I've always had a raspy, and squeaky voice and I often despised my child like voice. It wasn't until God reassured me my voice is a blessing and not a hindrance and it doesn't take away from what I was called to do. Your voice is a communication between your heart and the rest of the world. Don't be afraid to be heard.

Pearls of Wisdom for Aspiring Entrepreneurs

- **Don't compare your beginnings to established entrepreneurs.** Building businesses takes time to. Your appointed time is your appointed time. The posture of your heart will align with where it's meant to be along as your intentions are pure.

- **Identify viable working plans for strategically marketing your business.** Stay in tune with your customer base. Have you tried selling or offering a product? Has it failed? Who is your target audience? Are they engaged? Establish an accountability partner to boost your productivity and get rid of dead business weight timely.

- **Become comfortable with your voice.** Your voice is an important attribute to your brand. The world needs to hear from you. It sets the tone for the foundation of your brand.

- **Don't be afraid to ask for assistance or hire help.** Some entrepreneurs are excited to help other entrepreneurs. Some may say no, but that's still ok. Understand though that help doesn't equal an endorsement.

- **Dare to be different.** If you're selling t-shirts or remote controls, what makes yours any different from your competition? Why should a consumer buy from you and what makes yours so special? Present something in a different context so they can't say they've heard this pitch before.

- **Maintain a clear and concise appearance to your brand.** Your brand should have some type of uniformity. Make it neat and engaging.

- **Realizing your competition but staying professional.** What's meant for you, is for you…period.

Common Mistakes Entrepreneurs Make

- **Cookie cutting ideas.** You can't take another company's concept and expect to manifest your business from someone else's vision. Realize the difference between being inspiring and simply copying someone else's idea.

- **Not capturing your target audience.** Identify the *"who"*, *"why"* and *"what"* of your company. Who are you? Why was the company founded? What message do you want conveyed to your audience?

- **Identify the needs of your audience.** What will your audience walk away with? Will it help them? What problem are you solving for them? Will they recommend and refer your business?

- **Not creating a memorable presentation.** When I ship tees for *Single Mothers for Christ*, I enclose a personalized handwritten thank you card to each customer, a copy of my business card and a beautiful reusable bag which reflects the (staple color of my company). Take pride in the product you're offering. You only get one chance to make a first impression.

- **Not maintaining statics of performance of services.** Identify what's working and what's not working. Was your audience engaged? Did it prompt your audience to share?

- **Begging for shouts outs!** You don't have to beg anyone to support you. Divine relationships will come from God, not your efforts.

- **Not investing in your appearance.** If you're the face of the company, do you have quality professional headshots? Selfies or photos taken on your cell phone simply will not work *if* you want to be taken seriously.

- **Quality graphics!** If you want to advertise something, make the investment to purchase a quality flyer. Graphics are an investment but are well worth it because they are the representation of your brand. Make them exciting from the moment your post.

Remember*: All things are working for your good!*
(Romans 8:28)

Connect with Cierra Michelle:
Facebook/Instagram: Cierra Michelle
Twitter: @RealCMichelle

Schan Ellis is a spiritual life coach whose vision is to co-create a consciously enlightened world, where we tap into our authentic power through self-exploration, discovery of possibilities and a willingness to do a new thing in order to awaken our greatness! Schan's style is unconventional and intentionally designed to support clients in expanding beyond comfort zones to experience life in a greater way. This is EmpowHERed Living!

Your Brand Story Matters:
Write Your Story Beautiful

My journey to entrepreneurship does not have big bells and whistles. It was something I just literally stepped into. No plan or nothing. It's funny now, but it's exactly what I did. I had already identified my gift of writing and knew for years I had been writing web content for businesses, voiceover scripts for pastors, special events programs for churches, proofing and editing company print marketing material, etc.

I did all of this for free simply because I loved doing it and quite frankly didn't know any better to even charge or demand a price for my services. In a sense, although my services were being highly sought after, I didn't see myself as an "expert" or value the gift enough to transform it into a viable, profitable business. Now fast forward to 2011 when I published my first book. During the process, I had to activate my critical thinking skills. I had to take into consideration the cost of publishing and printing, using that to come up with a price point that would allow me to recoup my expenses and make a profit.

It forced me to create a marketing plan and prompted me to set up a Square account to accept credit/debit payments which led to me opening a business account. With just those few things in place, I found myself being successful with sales. I saw value in those humble beginnings which led me to begin to expound more in regard to my business. I consider myself a creative entrepreneur and I find great joy in keeping things simple.

I particularly enjoy the lightness of allowing things to flow freely, learning from my mishaps, evaluating the progress, keeping things that worked and implementing new mastery tools that have been proven successful. I know this is unconventional and may not work for everyone, however, it has worked for me and all or part of it may work for you as well.

Once I started believing in myself to have a thriving business here are three value points I began with:

> **1**. I began to pray, asking God what direction my business should go in. I sought direction and focus from the master of creation. I implemented daily meditation and would look forward to being still, in silence and allowing great ideas to be poured into me. I've found that there's beauty in being still and waiting.

> **2**. As a child, I watched my mother be so serving to her family, our neighbors and even customers at her job. I watched how she interacted and how it seemed to give her great joy being of service to others. I knew that's the kind of feeling I wanted. So, I made sure that in my business, I

provided a service that not only mattered, but I wanted to serve my clients and give them more than what was expected.

3. I sought to build and solidify relationships through networking and creating visibility, both physically and socially. These relationships helped me on one hand to understand the beauty of support and the other hand, to bring clarity on who would not support or who wasn't great for business. Relationships are one of the keys to success.

That being said, I have learned that entrepreneurship is ever changing and because of that, each day I set my intention to learn, expand and evolve myself as a creative being, which directly effects the expansion and evolution of my business.

So, entrepreneurs, whether you are seasoned, young or aspiring, I have faith in you. God has already placed within you, greatness, gifts, and talents that you must use to multiply and replenish the earth. On this journey, don't be afraid of making mistakes. It's a part of mastery. As I learned from watching an animated movie recently, *"If you only do what you can do, you will never be more than you are now."* ~ Master Shifu, Kung Fu Panda. Be creative, stretch yourself and just step into it! Growth takes place outside of the box and outside of your comfort zone. PUSH through it and manifest your destiny!

Now fast forward and step on into my world. I'm honest, I'm human and I've made a whole lot of mistakes and probably will make more, although now, as I've learned, those mistakes should be fewer and further between.

Here are five clear mistakes I've made on this entrepreneurial journey.

1. **Giving away my products and services FREE without a strategic plan.** What I mean by that is, it's ok to offer free items...a workbook, eBook, coaching session, etc., however its strategic when you have a plan to turn those

free clicks into paying clients. I didn't have a strategy at first. I was Oprah giving away the goods! (Lol) We cannot reasonably desire high paying clients but discount prices to gain MORE customers rather than using competitive prices to attract the clients you want. If you offer a free service, make sure that you have created a way to capture their email address to later use to send marketing messages, exclusive sales offers, and other quick, free points of value.

2. **Trying to provide services to everybody.** Every product and service are not for everyone. I found myself marketing *everything* I had to offer to the *same* audience. Yes, you'll have a core group who will support you no matter what you produce, however in business, we must learn the art of not only defining our target market, but also segmenting it as well. For example, strategies on how to build a successful business may not appeal to the woman who wants coaching to help write her book. Therefore, I had to come up with effective ways to use my resources, segment my market and not over burden *everybody* with *everything.* Broadening your audience while finding a balance in your marketing plan is essential.

3. **Wasting too much time.** There are 24 hours in a day. I have a full-time job (8hrs) and slept six hours on a good night. Now what happened to the other 10 hours? That was enough time to define and develop another full-time venture. I had to really stop and take inventory of my time. A lot of it was scrolling through Facebook, watching recorded television shows, texting, going out to eat somewhere or accepting *every* invitation to attend someone's event. All of those things can be draining and claim much of the capacity to be creative even if you tried. And I attempted all of the above and it had my attention more than my desire to launch my own business. If I wanted to be an entrepreneur and take this thing seriously, I

had to stop being a time waster. I had to make moments count. Becoming organized allowed me to do that. Maximizing my day has allowed me to give the needed attention to build my business, focus on my brand, be a leader in my community, make memories with my family, support others and most importantly take time for myself. It's a funny thing that when you get organize and implement strategies, you can accomplish more with less strain.

4. **Trying to do it all alone.** I knew the definition of delegating however, I didn't delegate well. I wanted to hold on and have control over every single detail which eventually led to frustration which finally led to just not getting tasks done. Not making moves at all meant business was not moving in the direction I desired. When we can lessen the need to be in total control and rather use that energy to delegate (choose wisely) and oversee tasks, then we can get more accomplished. It frees us up to focus on other areas of business.

5. **No hiring a mentor/coach early on.** I have BA in Business and Marketing, so this business thing should be a piece of cake, right? Not! Sure, there's much free information on the internet but there are some details and experiences you won't get from searching a computer screen or listening to free webinars and conference calls. I'm not knocking that at all. I used all those free services to my advantage until I was able to make this type of investment into my business. Sometimes you need face to face interactions, hands on training, knowledge, and wisdom from someone who has walked your path and lastly someone to actually hold you accountable. My business coach did just that for me. She provided valuable information from not only just teaching business at a university but also as a successful entrepreneur.

These lessons I've learned along the way have helped me to establish better business relationships and partnerships. I've also learned to create better brand stories, respect, and value my time, which is a commodity that once it's spent, it doesn't recycle.

Here are the mistakes I have witnessed other entrepreneurs make

Mistakes are simply missteps on your journey whether that be in life, personal relationships and yes, also in business. These missteps serve as learning tools on how *not* to do something the same way again. Not only that, but they should also serve as catalysts to keep going and to kick in gear the childhood lesson of *practice makes perfect*. Mistakes when evaluated produce experts and masters of your craft.

Below are a few mistakes that I have noticed with entrepreneurs from being on the consumer's side of the supply and demand spectrum. Although I am identifying error in other entrepreneurs, trust I've made some of the same ones therefore, I want to help prevent you from doing the same. It is my intention to share what I have experienced along with exploring, discovering, and creating solutions that work.

1. **"The best brands are built on great stories."** ~ Ian Rowden, Chief Marketing Officer, Virgin Group. Who are you? What do you sell? How does this product relate to me? Why do I need your service? All of this is contained within your brand story and to the consumer and should neither be questionable nor inconsistent. You brand story consists of every element of your business, including colors, business cards, the look and feel of your website, and staff. It should all relate to each other and in some way connect all five senses of touch, taste, smell, hear, see. When businesses develop a brand story, it should be built with a foundation in mind and a strategy for future growth and

expansion. Your brand story should spark an emotion, (albeit a positive one) when the consumer hears your name or sees your business. You want them to not only like your product but love it! You do this by creating a story that will differentiate you from your competitors, connecting you to the consumer with emotions which will ultimately boost your brand awareness, customer loyalty and increase your profits.

2. **"Advertising is just one part of your marketing plan. If that's the primary pillar of your marketing strategy, then you're doing it wrong."** ~ Kurt Uhlir, CEO & Founder of Sideqik. How often have we seen businesses border or cross the lines of spamming by tagging you in Facebook advertising posts or slamming your inbox with repeated messages to buy their product or service. While advertising can be beneficial when done strategically, it is not and should not be the complete foundation of your marketing plan. While there are several components to the marketing plan, one key element is relationship building. This enables you to connect with your target market and allows you the opportunity to connect with your brand story. Take for example McDonald's, they have created such a powerful brand story that they could simply display a mother eating a happy meal with her son without any mention of price or written message that says *"Go buy this happy meal."* McDonalds has built a great brand story and includes more than just advertising in their marketing plan.

3. **"Boost your visibility, build your audience. Build your audience, serve more people."** ~ Denise Wakeman, Adventures in Visibility. Recently I wanted to potentially do business with a photographer. He posted great pictures, so I wanted to explore further by visiting his website or sending him an email inquiry. That information wasn't

listed on his personal Facebook page. I also did an internet search for his business name, and nothing came up. I wanted to know his prices, see his portfolio, decide between packages, etc. Typically, if I haven't established a relationship with you, I rarely do business via your personal Facebook inbox. I want to feel that you are serious about your business (and you very well could be, but your visibility does not appeal to my five senses I talked about in creating your brand story) and that I can be secure in doing business with you. If you are unable to afford a website now, create a Facebook business page which is free and start posting your products there along with your personal page. If you are unable to afford a business phone number, you can get a Google number which is free and it connects right along with your personal mobile number and lastly, create business email. My business email is schan@schanellis.com, however, before I was able to invest in a professional website, my email address was bebeautifullyinspired@gmail.com, which again was free. There is a myriad of free resources available for you to be visible. We want to see you, your brand!

4. **"Your customer doesn't care how much you know, until they know how much you care."** ~ *Damon Richards, The Peaceful Entrepreneur.* My primary business is consulting and coaching. Clients come to me with their ideas and information, believing that I will help them to create a story that works for them. My intention is to make them feel valued and believe that their ideas and information they bring to the table matters. I am simply in place to enhance it. We can make our consumers feel valued by a.) Simply saying it. b) Showing it by exceeding your consumer's expectations. c.) Validate their decision even if you do not agree with them, d.) Always leave them

feeling positive about the service or product you've provided. I believe that business ultimately is not about what you sell, but rather more about the people you serve and the experience you provide. If we're honest, most products and services can be purchased anywhere. It's your unique experience that will create trust and loyalty in the long run.

5. **"The GREATEST Silent Killer of ALL Business: INCONSISTENCY."** Soomin-Kim,   The   Network Marketing Ninja. If you ask me something that I loathe in business, it would definitely be inconsistency. I can't stand it! In order for anything to grow or reach its full potential, you have to be consistent. A flower needs consistent watering to thrive, cookies need consistent heat to bake properly, a business needs consistent strategies to grow and expand. Develop a mindset of consistency. Some areas in your business you can develop consistency is a.) If you operate from 9am-5pm, be available. If you schedule an appointment with a client, show up and be on time and ready to work. Consistently not being there when you say you are, is a sure way for consumers to lose trust in you. b.) Your pricing should be fair and marketable. People will recognize when they are being ripped off and they will not feel good about it. c.) The level of service you provide should be welcomed and expected. I love Chick Fil A's service consistency. No matter what Chick Fil A I've gone to in the country I am expecting the same level of customer service and I'm never disappointed. d.) Your marketing plan, including the advertisement you send and the partnerships you enter should be consistent with your brand story. I can remember a time when I was asked by a particular company who sells products that were sexual in nature, to be guest speaker at a women's empowerment

brunch. I knew the brand story of this company from their Facebook posts however, maybe they were taking their brand in a different direction with this brunch. My brand story is about inspiration and empowerment and my messages are all clear with this story. As I continued to ask questions about the agenda and flow of the brunch, I discovered that afterwards there were going to be strippers and sexual products on display. Can you imagine photos being posted and video being recording with the *Be Beautifully Inspired* lady all up in the mix of this sex party? (Lol) While I don't knock the business, it was something that wasn't consistent with my story therefore, I politely declined. Be consistent, build your confidence and create a business that will develop brand recognition and connect consumers with your story. It's all about your story!

Connect with Schan B. Ellis Today!
Instagram/Twitter: @SincerelySchan
Facebook: Schan B. Ellis
www.Schanellis.com

Chapter 5
The Danger of Chasing More Than One Rabbit

W hile in pursuit of your destiny it can be very tempting to go after more than one venture at a time. One of the ways many remain stuck and never move forward is because they tend to pursue more than one thing at a time. One of the keys to success is the ability to follow one course until successful. This is the definition of the word, "FOCUS":

F-OLLOW

O-NE

C-OURSE

U-NTIL

S-UCCESSFUL

One of the things I heard media mogul, Tyler Perry say one day was too often people are chasing more than one opportunity at a time which in return causes them to have divided focus. WOW! Did you hear that? *Divided* focus. He then gave the example of when someone chases two rabbits and in doing so, they catch neither!

Whenever you are in pursuit of your destiny you must be laser focused on one project at a time and allow it to develop and expand before putting your hands into another endeavor. Divided focus equals no focus at all. This is also true regarding any endeavor you set out to do in life overall. Before you do anything, it is important to think it through and develop a strategic plan of action. The reason why so many people lose momentum while in pursuit of their destiny is because they did not have a predetermined mindset on *what* they intend to do, *why* they desire to do it and *how* they intend to do it.

Take a moment and answer the following questions:

1. What is it that you desire to do in life?

2. Why do you desire to do it?

3. How do you intend to make this desire a reality?

4. How do you intend to profit from your passion?

Before you step out into any business venture it's important to know the answers to the above questions. One of the greatest concerns I have witnessed aspiring entrepreneurs express is *"I am unsure how I can replace my income."*

Another thing I want you to do is write down every idea you have as it relates to being an entrepreneur:

1.
2.
3.
4.
5.

Now that you have identified the things you desire to do (you may have more than ten but that's okay) I'd like for you to now break that list down into five:

1.
2.
3.
4.
5.

Now that you have created your top 5 list, I want you to identify the top three:

1.

2.

3.

Now that you have created your top 3 list, I want you to identify the top two:

1.

2.

3.

Now I want you to think long and hard before doing this next activity of identifying the one (1) thing. I want you to dig deep within and identify, *'What it is you really want to do?'* During VIP sessions for my Fire your Boss Self-Study Coaching Program I have my clients answer the following question: *"What would you do if money was not an issue?"*

Answering the above question and listing it below will help you pursue your passion from a pure place rather than anxiety and fear.

I once had a coach tell me when I was in pursuit of full-time entrepreneurship: *"Carla, you don't have a money problem. You have an idea problem."* This was during a time that I was struggling and not sure how I was going to replace my income.

This gentleman was absolutely correct! I didn't have a money issue, but I needed to learn how to properly profit from my passion. I needed to learn how to bring my ideas into execution.

As I mentioned earlier, one of the keys to success is to become laser focused on one task at a time and follow it until completion. It is very important to not allow new trends and ideas to take you off your course nor alter the current plan of action you have in place.

One of the major differences from when I worked a 9 to 5 while running my business versus when I became a full-time entrepreneur was learning the importance of filling my calendar with "Profitable Activities."

For example: Some may view spending time on social media as a "Non-Productive Activity" which in some cases may be true. However, building relationships are essential to building your business. Why? Because people only buy from who they know, like and trust. This is why I have what I call a *"Love-em Up List"* within my business.

You may be wondering what that is. It is simply a list that I create after someone expresses interest in coaching, one of my programs or even book publishing. Once per week I connect with them to inquire about *them* not necessarily my services. When people see that you care and are not simply trying to sell them something they are more likely to invest in your program rather than going with someone else. The reason for this is because you expressed concern about them as a person and was willing to share some information for free that they can now! Once they see that small bit of advice work, they will run to you with their credit cards asking, *"Where do I sign up?"* Ha! I also call this *Strategic Marketing.*

When you are on social media, I encourage you to be intentional about the statuses you like, the comments you make as well as the posts you share. I would go even as far as saying be careful not to allow new social media outlets such as Periscope to cause you to lose focus of your ultimate mission.

Some people spend their entire day posting on social media and sharing statuses, as well as watching Periscope video after periscope video without gaining any knowledge of how to grow and expand their business. If you are going to watch Periscope or scroll on social media let it be during your down time not during the time you should be executing your business.

Or if you are going to tune into someone live via Periscope or even Facebook live then be sure it is something you can benefit from now. If not, do like I do and remain focused during the day and catch up on all your favorite *'scopers'* or tweets during your down time. Again, it's about being laser focused. Divided focus = No focus.

I also would like to encourage you to be intentional with every connection as well as every social media outlet you use. I intentionally follow individuals whom I can gain spiritual or professional knowledge from. I share posts of my clients and women I am connected with to show them that I support them and that their support of my movement/brand is not one sided.

I intentionally go on my Apostle's social media pages and "like" her statuses as well as my closest friends, clients, and colleagues to show them that I support them. I also share information they post because in doing this I am *nurturing* my relationships.

Facebook has an option for you to not only be friends with someone but also for you to follow them. Meaning if you follow them, you have the option to choose "See First" meaning you want their posts to show up in your news feed.

Now I don't recommend you do this for everyone, but I do encourage you to ensure those closest to you, within your network or even those within what I call "SISTER CIRCLE" posts are showing up in your newsfeed.

Individuals I intentionally follow and remain plugged into via Periscope are Bishop R.C. Blakes, Bishop Samuel Blakes, John Hannah, Apostle John Eckhardt, Dr. Matthew Stevenson and a few others. I do my best not to listen to too many voices at once. This is the number one way to get yourself in a continual spinning cycle going nowhere fast by having too many voices saying different things into your ear gate.

One of the things I am big on is knowing the voices that are assigned to you. I do not jump from Periscope to Periscope, nor do I sit on Facebook all day but I plug my content into www.hootsuite.com and I hop on during my down time to reply to my supporters (you may call them *followers*) as well as like a few statuses here and there.

In case you haven't learned yet, people take social media rather seriously. Therefore, maybe even instead of deleting or blocking people you can simply "Unfollow" them, so their posts do not show up in your newsfeed. Just to keep the peace. However, there are some instances where you clearly need to Unfriend them and it's okay to let them know it. Ha!

Maybe you have a colleague whose connection is vital to you, but you hate their posts. By blocking or deleting them on social media could hurt your relationship, however, clicking the "Unfollow" button would be much wiser.

Along this entrepreneur journey you will learn that your level of success is contingent upon (1) Your faith and obedience to God and (2) The relationships you intentionally develop and nurture.

Another profitable activity for me as an entrepreneur is communicating consistently (not in an overbearing manner) with my email list (these are people who have opt in (signed up through my website who have requested to receive information from me.) I share free tips, tools and strategies that help equip aspiring and current Kingdom Entrepreneurs on how to operate more effectively in the marketplace.

Another profitable activity I commit to doing daily is I share valuable information to my supporters on social media platforms such as Periscope (you can follow me @CarlaRCannon.) Monday-Friday I conduct free teachings which I call: *Daily Entrepreneur Tips* where I develop marketable titles and share pearls of wisdom over a course of 30-45 minutes.

Now you may ask, *'How is this a profitable activity?'* As a Kingdom Entrepreneur I am not afraid to share what I do and how it will benefit others. That is one reason why so many people do not profit within their business endeavors because (1) they are so busy chasing too many rabbits that no one can tell what service they are offering or (2) they lack the confidence needed to show up big, full of confidence and un-apologetically share what solution they are offering to the problem their clients are facing.

As an entrepreneur it is important that you be intentional in all that you do especially by monitoring time spent on social media. I joined Periscope in August 2015 and within a six-month time frame I made over $8,000 from *new clients.*

Now to some that may be a low number and they may be saying I made that in one day Carla. Well, for me and the current place I was in as an entrepreneur to use a new outlet such as Periscope to accumulate $8,000 as one *additional* stream of income is rather commendable.

While many entrepreneurs use social media to "pimp" people into buying their products by sharing no real content, I chose to first nurture my audience, spend time with them and allow them to learn my heart before I ever pitched a product or recommended one of my books.

I used other social media outlets in which my "tribe" had already been nurtured such as Twitter, Instagram and Facebook and shared valuable content such as hosting free webinars and pitching my coaching program at the end. I was careful not to do this initially on Periscope because I understand people only buy from who they know, like and trust. Periscope allowed me to attract and engage with an entirely different audience.

Other entrepreneurs may not agree with my methods, but this book is simply me sharing how I developed my darkest storms into a thriving business and how others can too. There is more than one way to success, and many are struggling to find their way and it is my hope that this book be of great help to and for them.

Below I'd like for you to fill in the chart and identify your current "Profitable Activities" and "Non-Profit Activities."

The key to this is to be honest and if you are currently working a 9 to 5 but are in pursuit of transitioning into a full-time entrepreneurship it is vital that you identify this *now* to prevent you from wasting precious time on activities that are not helping increase your bottom line in the future.

Think about the course of each day and identify tasks you do that generate income and those that do not. Remember to refer back to the examples I shared within this chapter.

Profitable Activities	Non-Profitable Activities

The purpose of having you complete the above activity is so you can experience a shift in your mindset and fill your calendar with things that bring you closer to your ultimate dream, goal, and vision.

As you learned in chapter 4 of this book it is vitally important for aspiring entrepreneurs to spend time preparing for the success they desire within their business.

On the contrary, individuals must be careful not to spend so much time preparing that they never activate or execute the plan of action they have in place.

Another purpose of completing the above activity is to help you become laser focused on the task at hand rather than pursuing multiple endeavors at a time. One thing I do to help keep me focused is I jot down ideas I receive in what I call a "catch all" notebook. This notebook is where I pencil my dreams, goals, thoughts and even my ideas. Things I desire to see manifested are written in this notebook along with ideas I receive.

Before implementing them, I write them down, shut my notebook, pray about it and then 24-48 hours I come back to it to see if I still have the same level of excitement. If yes, I may feel led to implement a new product, coaching program; etc. If not, I shelf it and eventually throw it out, recommend it to someone else or implement it during another season of my life.

Be careful not to try to pursue every thought that crosses your mind. I conducted a teaching via Periscope entitled, "The Mishaps of Multi-Tasking" and what I mentioned is the danger of being a jack of all trades and a master of none.

As an entrepreneur it is important for you to remember this: *"A confused mind will never buy."* This is so true. Have you ever been on a website and there were so many different options that you became so overwhelmed to the point that you didn't purchase anything?

You don't want people to feel that way when they come to your website. By the way, if you are an entrepreneur, you need a "hub" or place to direct all traffic to connect with you and opt into your website. Usually, you provide a free product or resource in exchange for a prospect's name and email address.

Be encouraged and know that entering entrepreneurship can be scary and at times feel overwhelming. But remember the best way to eat an elephant is simply by taking it one bite at a time.

Chapter 6
Characteristics of a Kingdom Entrepreneur

When it comes to pursuing your passion, I want you to take a moment and think of the current job/career you have and answer the following questions:

1. Are you happy on your job?

   YES or NO

2. Do you believe you are currently operating in your divine purpose?

   YES or NO

I intentionally wrote this book for aspiring entrepreneurs because there were not a lot of information shared as it relates to Kingdom Entrepreneurship. You may be asking, *"What is a Kingdom Entrepreneur?"*

"A Kingdom Entrepreneur is someone who has fully submitted and committed both their natural and supernatural gifts for the advancement of the Kingdom of God through the marketplace."

A Kingdom Entrepreneur is one whose ultimate priority is to make Jesus famous within the marketplace without a spirit of compromise. Some people do things for personal advancement; to make their names great or for monetary gain. As an entrepreneur it's important that money NOT be your driving force.

Having a spiritual and scriptural foundation is essential to ensure the success of a Kingdom Entrepreneurship.

When you properly align your business with God's word and agenda success will be inevitable. I believe strongly in connecting with mentors in the marketplace, but we must be careful not to allow their principles and strategies to replace our first line of duty which is to be stewards of the Word of God which is our ultimate blueprint for success.

Kingdom Entrepreneurs look to the Word of God to lead and guide them as it relates to how they conduct their business. The key to ensure your business is a success is by dedicating time daily to become a better person overall. This is established in prayer. Make a commitment to pray for your business and staff daily. Prayer really is the principal thing.

As it relates to entrepreneurship, so many people spend so much time working on their business rather than building up the person who is running the business. Personal development is key in this hour, and it is vital that you commit to becoming the best version of you by becoming a person of character, integrity and one who is in full pursuit of their destiny.

I believe strongly that whatever kind of spouse or friend we are is the same kind of business partner we will be. If you talk too much in your personal relationships, you'll talk too much in your business/partnerships. If you don't keep your word in your personal relationships, you will carry over the same traits in your business/professional life.

If you are negative, full of gossip and have backstabbing tendencies in your personal relationships you will bring that same negative energy and bad habits into your professional life.

Many people are struggling today to balance the finances within their business and that is because they never took the time to develop the practical skills needed to properly negotiate their personal finances.

As a Kingdom Entrepreneur it is vital that we look to the principles found in God's word to uplift a standard in our personal and professional life.

There is a website I want to refer you to that will help you tremendously as it relates to how to apply your spiritual gifts with business deals, negotiations, and endeavors. It is: https://www.facebook.com/ChurchforEntrepreneurs/?fref=ts. It is *Church for Entrepreneurs* and you can "like" this page on Facebook and signup to receive the podcasts directly to your email. It is a great site that offers encouragement specifically for Christian entrepreneurs.

Next, I want to share qualities of a Kingdom Entrepreneur. Within the table below you will see character traits that Kingdom Entrepreneurs possess (or should) as well why each character trait is necessary.

Character Traits of a KE:	**Why This Trait is Necessary:**
Trustworthy	People only buy from who they know, like & trust
Effective Communicator	To properly service your clients, you must *listen* more and speak less. It also must be crystal clear the type of services you provide. A confused mind will *never* buy!
Loyalty	Many people have been burned therefore, ensuring they understand that you are committed to their success will bring a sense of comfort.

Honest	If you are promoting a product or service, ensure that you are providing exactly what you say. It's better to over deliver than to under deliver. We call this creating greater value for your services where clients get more than they bargained for.
Positive Attitude	In all situations it's important to be positive and help others see the brighter side of things. People are always seeking encouragement and to be empowered. Positive energy, positive attitude and positive words are key!

Forbes.com records 10 qualities every leader must possess. They are the following:

(Here is the exact site in which you can reference at your leisure: *http://www.forbes.com/sites/tanyaprive/2012/12/19/top-10-qualities-that-make-a-great-leader/#9831ef356485)*

1. **Honesty-** Whatever ethical plane you hold yourself to, when you are responsible for a team of people, it's important to raise the bar even higher. Your business and its employees reflect yourself, and if you make honest and ethical behavior a key value, your team will follow suit.

2. **Delegate-** Finessing your brand vision is essential to creating an organized and efficient business, but if you don't learn to trust your team with that vision, you might never progress to the next stage. It's important to remember that trusting your team with your idea is a sign of strength, not weakness. Delegating tasks to the appropriate

departments is one of the most important skills you can develop as your business grows. The emails and tasks will begin to pile up, and the more you stretch yourself thin, the lower the quality of your work will become, and the less you will produce.

The key to delegation is identifying the strengths of your team and capitalizing on them. Find out what each team member enjoys doing most. Chances are if they find that task more enjoyable, they will likely put more thought and effort behind it. This will not only prove to your team that you trust and believe in them but will also free up your time to focus on the higher-level tasks, that should not be delegated. It's a fine balance, but one that will have a huge impact on the productivity of your business.

3. **Communication-** Knowing what you want accomplished may seem clear in your head, but if you try to explain it to someone else and are met with a blank expression, you know there is a problem. If this has been your experience, then you may want to focus on honing your communication skills. Being able to describe clearly and succinctly what you want done is extremely important. If you can't relate your vision to your team, you won't all be working towards the same goal.

Training new members and creating a productive work environment all depend on healthy lines of communication. Whether that stems from an open-door policy to your office, or making it a point to talk to your staff on a daily basis, making yourself available to discuss interoffice issues is vital. Your team will learn to trust and depend on you and will be less hesitant to work harder.

4. **Confidence-** There may be days where the future of your brand is worrisome, and things aren't going according to plan. This is true with any business, large or small, and the most important thing is not to panic. Part of your job as a

leader is to put out fires and maintain the team morale. Keep up your confidence level and assure everyone that setbacks are natural, and the important thing is to focus on the larger goal. As the leader, by staying calm and confident, you will help keep the team feeling the same. Remember, your team will take cues from you, so if you exude a level of calm damage control, your team will pick up on that feeling. The key objective is to keep everyone working and moving ahead.

5. **Commitment-** If you expect your team to work hard and produce quality content, you're going to need to lead by example. There is no greater motivation than seeing the boss down in the trenches working alongside everyone else, showing that hard work is being done on every level. By proving your commitment to the brand and your role, you will not only earn the respect of your team but will also instill that same hardworking energy among your staff. It's important to show your commitment not only to the work at hand, but also to your promises. If you pledged to host a holiday party, or uphold summer Fridays, keep your word. You want to create a reputation for not just working hard, but also be known as a fair leader. Once you have gained the respect of your team, they are more likely to deliver the peak amount of quality work possible.

6. **Positive Attitude-** You want to keep your team motivated towards the continued success of the company and keep the energy levels up. Whether that means providing snacks, coffee, relationship advice, or even just an occasional beer in the office, remember that everyone on your team is a person. Keep the office mood a fine balance between productivity and playfulness.

7. **Creativity-** Some decisions will not always be so clear-cut. You may be forced at times to deviate from your set course and make an on-the-fly decision. This is where your

creativity will prove to be vital. It is during these critical situations that your team will look to you for guidance, and you may be forced to make a quick decision. As a leader, it's important to learn to think outside the box and refuse to remain stuck. Don't immediately choose the first or easiest possibility; sometimes it's best to give these issues some thought, and even turn to your team for guidance. By utilizing all possible options before making a rash decision, you can typically reach the end conclusion you were aiming for.

8. **Intuition-** When leading a team through uncharted waters, there is no roadmap on what to do. Everything is uncertain, and the higher the risk, the higher the pressure. That is where your natural intuition must kick in. Guiding your team through the process of your day-to-day tasks can be honed down to a science. But when something unexpected occurs, or you are thrown into a new scenario, your team will look to you for guidance. Drawing on past experiences is a good reflex, as is reaching out to your mentors for support. Eventually though, the tough decisions will be up to you to decide, and you will need to depend on your gut instinct for answers. Learning to trust yourself is as important as your team learning to trust you.

9. **Inspire-** Creating a business often involves a bit of forecasting. Especially in the beginning stages of a startup, inspiring your team to see the vision of the successes to come is vital. Make your team feel invested in the accomplishments of the company. Whether everyone owns a piece of equity, or you operate on a bonus system, generating enthusiasm for the hard work you are all putting in is so important. Being able to inspire your team is great for focusing on the future goals, but it is also important for the current issues. When you are all mired deep in work, morale is low, and energy levels are fading, recognize that everyone needs a break now and then. Acknowledge the

work that everyone has dedicated and commend the team on each of their efforts. It is your job to keep spirits up, and that begins with an appreciation for the hard work.

10.**Approach-** Not all human beings are the same. A basic concept, but something that is often overlooked. You have cultural perspectives, language barriers, different educational backgrounds, personality traits and varying value systems with which individuals come pre-conditioned that greatly affects how information is processed and interpreted. Some people work well under pressure, others don't. Some respond best to tough love; others take it personally and shut down. To optimize your effectiveness as a leader, you must have the ability to customize your approach on a person-by-person basis, based on the situation at hand. Your capacity to execute this concept will play a huge role in your ability to get the best work out of your team and other partners along the journey.

As you can see success is not as the world tells us, "On our own terms." But success is submitting to God's way and being a person of our word, doing right by others and surrendering every gift we have to Christ and allowing Him to multiply and expand it!

That is one of the things I am believing the Lord for in this hour: to enlarge our capacity especially as ministers and Kingdom Entrepreneurs. Far too long we have accepted the world's way of telling us what real success is, which is when they equate it to temporal things such as: the amount of money in your bank account, the type of house you live in or car you drive.

But that is not the true definition of success at all. True success to me, is identifying why you were created (your purpose) and developing and implementing a strategy to walk it out in your everyday life (vision.)

Take a moment to define success on your own terms below:

Success to me means

_____

_____

_____

_____

_____

_____

Purpose is *why* we were created, and vision is *how* we plan to walk out the very reason for our existence. One of the most powerful books I've read that will help you tremendously in this area is: *The Principles and Power of Vision* by the late great Dr. Myles Munroe.

Here's how Dr. Munroe describes vision: *"Vision is a source of hope; it's the source of courage; it's the source of perseverance in the midst of difficulty."*

Before you can set out to do anything whether it is to identify your purpose, launch a business, become the best version of yourself; no matter what it may be from personal to professional goals you must have a predetermined mindset that success is indeed your portion; and failing is not an option for you.

The purpose of this book is for you to use this as a reference guide and be reminded that no matter what you desire to do in life there are thousands of others that have gone before you. Success leaves clues and if they can do it, then surely you can too!

Chapter 7
Pearls of Wisdom for Entrepreneurs

Entrepreneur.com records pearls of wisdom Oprah Winfrey shared with their readers in which they have identified as **"24 Quotes on Success by Oprah Winfrey."**

Note: You may find the full article via this site: http://www.entrepreneur.com/article/269979. I chose to omit quote number 3 where Oprah talks about "luck" because as Kingdom Entrepreneurs we do not operate off a "luck system" but of a "God/Faith/Favor System."

I included Oprah's quotes because she shares great principles and as Kingdom Entrepreneurs, I believe it is important to cross reference and learn from those within and without the four walls of the church. I learn valuable lessons and principles from entertainers; etc. as well. The point is so can you! Oprah is an exceptional businesswoman who's early beginning did not appear that she would end up on the path she is on now and it is because she lives by the below qualities that "Oprah" has become a household name.

1. Find your calling.

"Everybody has a calling. And your real job in life is to figure out as soon as possible what that is, who you were meant to be, and to begin to honor that in the best way possible for yourself."

2. Dreams.

"The key to realizing a dream is to focus not on success but on significance -- and then even the small steps and little victories along your path will take on greater meaning."

3. Vision.

"Create the highest, grandest vision possible for your life, because you become what you believe."

4. Make a difference.

"You have to know what sparks the light in you so that you, in your own way, can illuminate the world."

5. Do your best.

"My philosophy is that not only are you responsible for your life but doing the best at this moment puts you in the best place for the next moment."

6. Know your purpose.

"You know you are on the road to success if you would do your job and not be paid for it."

7. Wealth.

"The reason I've been able to be so financially successful is my focus has never, ever for one minute been money."

8. Celebrate life.

"The more you praise and celebrate your life, the more there is in life to celebrate."

9. Follow your own path.

"Often we don't even realize who we're meant to be because we're so busy trying to live out someone else's ideas. But other people and their opinions hold no power in defining our destiny."

10. Choose excellence.

"The choice to be excellent begins with aligning your thoughts and words with the intention to require more from yourself."

11. Keep good company.

"Surround yourself with only people who are going to lift you higher."

12. Possibility.

"Understand that the right to choose your own path is a sacred privilege. Use it. Dwell in possibility."

13. Do what you love.

"Passion is energy. Feel the power that comes from focusing on what excites you."

14. Be the artist of your life.

"With every experience, you alone are painting your own canvas, thought by thought, choice by choice."

15. Leave your comfort zone.

"I believe that one of life's greatest risks is never daring to risk."

16. Make a difference.

"What material success does is provide you with the ability to concentrate on other things that really matter. And that is being able to make a difference, not only in your own life but in other people's lives."

17. Stay positive.

"I know for sure that what we dwell on is who we become."

18. Authenticity.

"I had no idea that being your authentic self could make me as rich as I've become. If I had, I'd have done it a lot earlier."

19. Be limitless.

"Every time you state what you want or believe, you're the first to hear it. It's a message to both you and others about what you think is possible. Don't put a ceiling on yourself."

20. Take risks.

"Do the one thing you think you cannot do. Fail at it. Try again. Do better the second time. The only people who never tumble are those who never mount the high wire. This is your moment. own it."

21. Growth.

"Turn your wounds into wisdom."

22. Follow your passion.

"What I know is, is that if you do work that you love, and the work fulfills you, the rest will come."

23. Take action.

"The big secret in life is that there is no big secret. Whatever your goal, you can get there if you're willing to work."

● ●

Emanuel James "Jim" Rohn was an American entrepreneur, author and motivational speaker. His rags to riches story played a large part in his work, which influenced others in the personal development industry. He passed away in 2009 however, he leaves behind a legacy in which www.Success.com is intentional in keeping his legacy going by sharing phenomenal teachings and quotes by Jim Rohn such as those listed below which were found at the above website:

10 Powerful Quotes by Jim Rohn

1. *"Don't wish it was easier, wish you were better. Don't wish for less problems, wish for more skills. Don't wish for less challenge, wish for more wisdom."*

2. *"The challenge of leadership is to be strong, but not rude; be kind, but not weak; be bold, but not a bully; be thoughtful, but not lazy; be humble, but not timid; be proud, but not arrogant; have humor, but without folly."*

3. *"We must all suffer one of two things: the pain of discipline or the pain of regret."*

4. *"Days are expensive. When you spend a day, you have one less day to spend. So, make sure you spend each one wisely."*

5. *"Discipline is the bridge between goals and accomplishment."*

6. *"If you are not willing to risk the unusual, you will have to settle for the ordinary."*

7. *"Motivation is what gets you started. Habit is what keeps you going."*

8. *"Success is nothing more than a few simple disciplines, practiced every day."*

9. *"Don't join an easy crowd; you won't grow. Go where the expectations and the demands to perform are high."*

10. *"Learn how to be happy with what you have while you pursue all that you want."*

Another great article I thought would add value to this book in relation to entrepreneurship was found at http://www.success.com/article/rohn-4-keys-to-unlock-the-power-of-your-mind entitled,

4 Keys to Unlock the Power of Your Mind

By: Jim Rohn

1. Change your beliefs.

Many people do not believe that they can learn, master knowledge, or become "smart." These are deeply held beliefs for many, and ultimately, if we do not believe it, we will not achieve it.

So, change your beliefs. It is up to you to do the work of changing your beliefs. And when you do, you will be opening new worlds—literally! Feed your mind with information that will change your belief. The truth is that you have an amazing mind with a capacity for learning that is beyond your comprehension. You must believe this. And when you do, you will be unlocking the potential of your mind.

2. Get the right knowledge.

What keeps some people from learning is that they choose not to access or do not have access to knowledge. Knowledge comes from experiences, books, people and other "knowledge dispensers." We must tap into that knowledge.

So, get the right knowledge. Words if they are not true are meaningless. I hear children say, "I read it in a book." But is it true? Just because someone says it or writes it, doesn't mean it is true. As a learner, you want to get the right knowledge, not just information or opinions. It is your job to seek out information and knowledge and then test it and run it through your mind to see if it is true, and if it can be rightfully applied to your life to make it better and help you succeed. You need to weigh and measure what you learn to gain the right knowledge. And when you do, you will be unlocking the potential of your mind.

3. Become passionate about learning.

Some people simply do not have the desire to learn. They may be lazy, or they may not see the positive impact that learning would have on them. They have no passion inside that drives them to learn.

So become passionate about learning. This will take some work, but the only way to do it is to begin learning about things that have an immediate impact in your life. When you learn about a new financial concept that helps you earn money or get out of debt that will get you fired up. When you learn about how to interact with your family in a healthy way and your relationships get better, that will inspire you. Become passionate about learning. And when you do, you will be unlocking the potential of your mind.

4. Discipline yourself through the hard work of study.

Gaining knowledge is hard work and takes a lifetime to master. It is an ongoing discipline that is never complete.

So, discipline yourself through the hard work of study. Learning will take work. Until someone comes up with modules that can plug into your mind and give you instant access to knowledge, you are on your own, and that takes work. The process of learning is a long one. Yes, we can speed it up, but it is still a process of reading, listening, reviewing, repetition, applying the knowledge, experiencing the outcomes, readjusting, etc. Simply put, that takes time. Slowly but surely, when you discipline yourself, you gain knowledge and learn. And when you do, you will be unlocking the potential of your mind.

Learning is possible, no matter what your age. You are never too young or too old. Your mind was created to learn and has a huge capacity to do so. This week, make a commitment to unlock the potential of your mind!

I encourage you to subscribe to SUCCESS Magazine and review www.Success.com as well as subscribe to Entrepreneur magazine at www.Entrpreneur.com. These are two magazines that I have added to my library, and I am on their websites faithfully researching and learning all I can about entrepreneurship as well as on becoming a better leader.

• •

Speaking of leadership, I could not mention leadership and not share pearls of wisdom from one of my favorite speakers, authors, and mentors of all time: John C. Maxwell. This guy is the epitome of the word "legacy." He has expanded the John Maxwell team literally across the world by training individuals on how to be great speakers, teachers, and leaders. This is what life is all about; mentorship and discipleship to ensure we don't go to the grave with our gifts but the more we learn we pour into others which will ensure we die empty; with our purpose being fulfilled.

Inc.com have compiled forty-four of what they have identified as John Maxwell's best quotes in relation to leadership: (the exact link in which I received the below information is http://www.inc.com/peter-economy/44-inspiring-john-c-maxwell-quotes-that-will-take-you-to-leadership-success.html. Be sure to check out this site and sign up for their newsletters. Be sure to also subscribe to yet another great magazine by visiting www.inc.com.

As you can see this book is for those who are serious about becoming more business savvy in order to properly position themselves to operate at their absolute best in all they set out to do in life. I say find your *sweet spot* then eat up! Meaning: Identify what works for you, what you are excellent at and do it to the best of your ability. Another way of saying it is to simply *stay in your lane!*

Chapter 8
How to Build Your Business While Working
a
9 to 5

As we come to the final chapters of this book, it is my goal to have equipped you with not only greater knowledge and wisdom as it relates to beginning or even furthering your vision as an entrepreneur, but to have painted a clear picture on the "How to."

So often we hear people telling us what to do while lacking the "How to" component. Here in this chapter, I would like to share step by step how I built a profitable brand and within 5 months of really being serious I was able to fire my boss and become my own COO.

Previously I shared my journey into entrepreneurship but this time I am going to share it from a different angle. With my story (history, place of origination or testimony as many of you may like to call it from the faith-based community) being one of judgment, rejection, hurt, pain and shame it was always my heart to help others feel or even experience a sense of belonging.

Growing up I always felt as if I did not fit. I didn't fit in school, with my family and forget about friends because I didn't have any of those (none that were what I've learned real friends are and should look like.)

In the midst of the adversity and dysfunction I originated from it's as if God Himself had placed a spirit of resilience and determination on the inside of me. Because each time I was told "No!" Or if when a teacher told me I'd never amount to anything, it's like I'd cry for that moment but then something would go off on the inside of me and I'd rise no matter how many times I was knocked down.

Here's the turning point my friend, and I pray it also becomes a turning point for you as it relates to transforming or developing your darkest storms into a thriving business: I took all my pain and broken pieces and began to speak life into others. At the time I had no one to tell me I could make it, or that I mattered. Or that I wasn't bossy but was created to be a leader. That I didn't just have the gift of gab but that I'd travel the world speaking in an effort to impact millions of people.

One day I used what I had to share the message that was burning in my heart which was my cell phone. I began to send out inspirational text to a group of people that were dear to me. What I did not know was that one act of obedience was the start of a major movement.

From that one day of sending inspirational texts, I began to send them out each day. I remember feeling as if I was operating in my purpose because I would receive responses such as, "Right on time!" Or "I really needed this today!" I knew then that it's not always the big things, but God often resides in the small things as well.

I remember for months I'd send out inspirational texts to friends, family and colleagues simply sharing a message of hope. Reminding them that God was in control. What I didn't realize is I was always on a mission to make Jesus famous, it's just often we get so caught up in the process that we forget to enjoy ourselves in the process.

After sending inspirational texts for some time, I began to type up personal letters and print them off on colorful paper and I would mail them to different people I was connected to. Often I would carry a few in my purse folded up and would give them to individuals whom I may have met in the grocery store or mall. While making small talk I'd hand it to them and tell them to read it at their leisure. The responses were always amazing.

Little did I know this movement had expanded and was really touching the hearts of the people. After mailing out these letters I remember placing these words at the top: Women of Standard. What a powerful name that is and the world would soon know about.

One day as I was stuffing the letters one by one into envelopes preparing to mail them out, my co-worker at the time noticed what I was doing. She stopped at my desk and asked, "Have you ever thought about putting that in newsletter format?" My response to her was, "Girl I don't know how to do that." With a small laugh she said, "I can do it for you. Send it to me." Not knowing where this would lead to, I shrugged and said, "What the heck…" So, I sent it to her and within moments she sent it back to me all beautiful in newsletter form with my picture on it and I'll never forget, it was my first newsletter, and it was front and back!

I remember seeing it and screaming because my one small vision had been brought to life with a little structure and graphics. I remember seeing my co-worker smile as I almost cried while saying, "You're welcome."

After that day, my co-worker designed my newsletter for me for the next eleven months free of charge! I couldn't believe it! One inspirational text message had developed into a one-page letter that then turned into a beautiful, multi-page newsletter. I did not skip a beat. I shared those newsletters everywhere! My mom was printing them off at her store and sharing them with everyone.

We shared them on Facebook, passed them out in the community and I'm telling you people were excited about receiving them every month. Guess what else? They were in full color. I used up a lot of my mom's ink and printer paper to keep this going every month.

What I didn't realize during it all is that I was building an empire one brick, one person, one day at a time. I was sharing a message of hope, love with others who were on the verge of giving up until they came across one of the articles in my newsletter. We were sharing it everywhere via email, social media, local community; etc.! It was so amazing! As I reflect on where it all began, I am so in awe of every person I met while in corporate America or during any time of my life. Each person was necessary and whether good or bad it all made me stronger, and I am a better more stable person today because of all of it.

Notice I said one of the articles. Ha! I grew from a one-page newsletter to a four-to-five-page newsletter with guest contributors, advertisement space and everything. What I didn't know is not only had I developed my ministry, but I was also learning how to think like a professional and profit from my passion.

That's a point to keep in mind: It is possible and perfectly okay to prosper from your passion. I do not live by the mentality that says, the poorer we are then the closer we are to God. I do not live by that philosophy. I believe that as Kingdom Entrepreneurs we never work for money, but we make our money work for us!

Guess what happened next? After writing the newsletter and distributing it for a year, one of my fellow brothers in ministry asked, "Why don't you start a magazine?" Now this time I laughed really hard and said, "What? I have no clue how to do that!" He said, "No worries. I'll design it for you."

Now you can imagine the emotions I felt because first I had a coworker offer to design a newsletter for me absolutely free and it was a very successful endeavor. Next, my friend is telling me he will develop my newsletter into a magazine. I was completely blown away by even the thought of it!

Long story short, I submitted the requested information to my friend, he then took it and developed it into a magazine and sent it to me. I can remember receiving the first box of fifty printed copies of my first ever magazine. I opened that box, held it in my hand and cried like someone had just sent me a million dollars in the mail and I didn't have to pay it back! Ha!

I remember flipping page by page, re-reading articles that I had edited but it was something different about reading it on my computer screen, or on loose pieces of paper. It was now in between a hard cover with phenomenal graphics that helped enhance the message.

We went on to create and distribute Women of Standard Magazine for over two years and during that time my mind began to expand, and I was committed to operating in excellence. In doing so, I was granted access to interview many prominent leaders in the Gospel arena from artists to speakers to authors and more. They included Yolanda Adams, Tasha Cobbs, Kierra Sheard, Stormie Omartian, Dr. Jamal Bryant, Hart Ramsey, JJ Hairston, VaShawn Mitchell, Lisa Page Brooks, Shirley Murdock and more!

What was my key to divine favor and success? (1) Dedication (2) Consistency (3) Excellence. I was not only dating the vision, but I was married to it. The more I began to step out in purpose, on purpose and was open to what Holy Spirit wanted to do in my life I experienced success after success.

(1) **Dedication:** Anything you pursue in life, for it and you to be successful you must be committed; dedicated to

following it through. Building your dream life will require dedication. You can't work on your vision today and then not touch it tomorrow. You must be (2) Consistent and determined to see it through! In order to do this, it will require FOCUS! I mentioned this in the previous chapter, but a reminder never hurt anybody therefore, here it is *again!*

F-OLLOW

O-NE

C-OURSE

U-NTIL

S-UCCESSFUL

The lack of focus is one thing that will dry up your level of creativity and cause you to lose momentum in your endeavors. You must decide that whatsoever you start you are going to see it all the way to the end. Guess what? As you become laser focused on your dream's distractions are going to pop up from everywhere to try and distract you!

You may get a nail in your tire that will require you to spend money you already don't have. Or you may receive a parent/teacher request from your kid's teacher because they were clowning in class. Or even worst (and God forbid) your spouse may come home and say, "This isn't working out. I'm leaving." No matter what happens, you must be determined to K.I.M. (Keep It Moving)

Refuse to allow any situation whether in your control or out of your control cause you to give up on your dreams of becoming an entrepreneur. Is it easy? No! Will it require sacrifice? Yes! Will it be worth it? Absolutely! Every financial sacrifice you make will be worth it! Every time you deny yourself of instant pleasure such as paying ten bucks to see a new movie at eight with all your friends, you may have to catch the matinee so you can pay half the price.

You may say, well it's only ten bucks geez Carla. But that ten bucks can lead you to ten grand! What if you spent twenty bucks on graphic design that could up-level your brand that will bring you five to ten clients at let's say.... $47 a person?

As an entrepreneur it's important that you make wise decisions and get a hold of your money now because if you are a lousy keeper of your finances as an employee, when your roles change you will be even worse as an employer or entrepreneur.

(3) Thirdly, you must be committed to operate in a spirit of excellence. As Kingdom Entrepreneurs we must spend more time planning for our success instead of thinking we are going to just step out on blind faith! No ma'am. No sir.

A goal without a strategic plan of action is simply a wish! Understand that if you fail to plan, then you must plan to fail-Winston Churchill. You must be committed to presenting your best self to the world. Refuse to back down from what you desire and go after what rightfully belongs to you!

Motivational Speaker and Author Les Brown said reach for the stars even if you miss, you'll land amongst the stars. I want to encourage you to dream again, go big again! Desire greatness again! Who killed your dreams? Who told you, you'd make no money doing that?

Could it be that it didn't work the last time because you lacked the proper strategy and you failed to include a financial plan that covers a monthly budget? Sometimes we give up the dream when it is the strategy that simply needs tweaking or altering. Refuse to give up in this hour. You may have to tweak some things or go back to the drawing board or even get rid of that plan altogether and start over but refuse to give up the vision although you may have to give up your present strategy for another.

Now one thing I did not mention amid sharing my compelling story of how I used natural gifts to develop a movement that is empowering the lives of thousands of people today! During running and operating Women of Standard Magazine with a full staff that consisted of an Administrative Assistant, Editor-In-Chief and over twenty contributors.

On top of that we had monthly team meetings with all contributors which consisted of me sharing an empowering message to ensure I kept my staff motivated as we discussed the magazine layout and features for the upcoming month. On top of that I had to meet separately with my executive team which was a challenge because when you have broad vision but others around you have tunnel vision that can put a lid on your dreams. What I learned quickly was although I had great Christians around me, they were not the ones God wanted to use to help carry this vision to where I saw and knew it could excel to.

But I knew I could not get rid of them and try to do this all on my own but with the financial pressure, individuals constantly meeting deadlines, running into technical errors with my web developer, trying to keep the printing cost down so we can continue to print the magazine and have it available in various cities I began to face burn out.

Understand this, no one will never be as fully invested into your business or ministry as you! This was a hard lesson I had to learn. Although I had people to my left and to my right standing with me, I was the only one busting my behind to ensure this was paid and that was paid, and that we had enough advertisement to cover the price of printing this month, then on top of that having to market and promote it to the world while a staff of individuals simply enjoy the ride while I do all the hard work.

Now this is not to throw any shade at any one and I am not salty about it at all. I am simply sharing with you my journey so you can be inspired and understand there may be things you start out doing that you don't end up doing. There may be people who start out with you but don't end up with you. They key is to always take a moment to breathe but then get right back in the ring.

Guess what else? I was doing all of this while I was still working my 9 to 5!!!! There it is!!! You have been waiting for it. I'm sure you thought, "Boy, Carla sure did miss it. This chapter has nothing to do with building your business while working a 9 to 5." Boy were you wrong! Ha!

As a writer it is my desire to not just throw knowledge at you but to take you on a journey into my life to share my successes as well as my failures for you to see that no one has this thing all figured out. Just like you, we too have to step out to find out! Did I know the magazine would be successful for over two years and develop into a brand in which we begin to host conferences, workshops, and networking events to connect other women together who are called from the pulpit to the marketplace?

Absolutely not! I had no clue, but I completed my course until I felt Holy Spirit say, okay now it's time to shift! Along with shifting comes sifting! You must understand the people who usually start out with you will not always go on with you. Now this may be a hard pill to swallow but guess what I need you to do: Chew Slow!

That's right, embrace this understanding that the guy you called your right hand just may betray you and want out of the partnership leaving you in all kinds of debt. Or to you my sister the very one who called you her Oprah and you called her your Gayle, she may not find your friendship worth fighting for and grow silent and just may stop answering your call.

Often times, people think money or success changes people when the truth is life should change all of us; for the better. You should desire to grow and excel in your business, ministry, friendships and even your relationships. If you have been dating a guy for a year and he hasn't mentioned marriage, it's okay to bring it up.

If you are carrying all the weight in your business while your partner sleeps all day while stuffing popcorn in his mouth and watching Netflix, yes, you should say something! Life happens to all of us, we all get knocked down. We all fall in a rut, but the key is to climb or fight your way out of that thing.

Listen, I had a very demanding job but in the midst of it my passion lied outside of my job. I was only there to receive a paycheck to help fund my business. This is why you can't be hasty and ready to up and quit your job without having a strategic plan of action on how you plan to replace your income on a consistent basis to cover your basic needs every month.

What are basic needs: shelter, lights, food, and clothes right? Now if you are like me, I add in my cell phone because that is how I conduct business. However, I can make it without cable. After years of sowing into certain ministries the Lord released me from doing that and I focused on tithing only in my local church and planting my financial seeds there.

That's another thing, as an entrepreneur you have to sow where you desire to go so that you can grow and refuse to give up in the process. Often times, we are smack dead in front of our desired life or expected goal and we run out of fuel for that final stretch, and we forfeit it all simply because we didn't pace ourselves.

Okay, now let's go back and dive into the real work. I shared with you that I built the Women of Standard brand over a course of four years while I worked my 9 to 5. In the mix of that I authored not one, not two, not three but four best-selling books! All while working my 9 to 5 (which are pictured in the back of this book.)

While working my 9 to 5 I was dedicated, committed, and completely married to the vision of building the Women of Standard brand, writing books, hosting annual conferences and workshops all while working a 9 to 5! If I can do it, you can do it!

If you are currently working a 9 to 5 and want to learn how to build your business in the process here are a few things I want you to keep in mind:

1. Remain focused!

2. Marry the vision

3. Be willing to sacrifice!

4. Sow where you want to go!

5. Make Kingdom Connections!

6. THINK. DREAM. GO BIG!

7. Refuse to Carry Others When You Can Barely Walk Yourself!

8. Take time to BREATHE!

9. Life is a marathon not a sprint!

10. Surround yourself with Winners so YOU can WIN!

BONUS: Play BIG not safe!

Chapter 9
Fire Your Boss & Hire Yourself as COO

The Entrepreneur Blueprint derived from my new self-study coaching program entitled, Fire Your Boss: A Six Step Guide to Transitioning into Full Time Entrepreneurship. The purpose of this program is to walk you through a step-by-step process that will prepare you psychologically, financially and spiritually for this big move! I am not going to lie to you and tell you that the path to entrepreneurship is easy. You can tell that from the previous chapters within this book and guess what else? There are no guarantees. But guess what else? Neither is your job!

I know you may have all kinds of thoughts going through your head such as, *"Can this really happen for me?" "Who am I kidding? There are no entrepreneurs in my family."* Or perhaps you feel a grip of fear hanging onto you that is trying to keep you bound in a traditional mindset of busting your butt working a job that you hate for years only to retire feeling unfulfilled and as if it was all a waste.

So many people remain stuck into thinking their job offers *security* which then causes them to shy away from the uncomfortable path of pursuing entrepreneurship full time because they are not sure what to expect. Truth is, no one's job is secure especially with today's economy. You could walk into your job tomorrow and be handed a pink slip with little to no explanation. Then what? Do you have a back-up plan in place? Do you have a plan B? Have you even thought about it?

My passion and heart is to help birth out entrepreneurs. This program is only for those who not necessarily hate their job but feel a sense of more. Often times we allow others to make us feel bad for desiring more out of life. Take a moment and declare aloud, "It is perfectly okay for me to desire more!" Your ultimate desire for more is what leads you into your life purpose. Now I am not the coach that will tell you to up and quit your job without having a structured plan in place, but I am one to encourage you to dare to take a risk.

Truth is there is no guarantee for any entrepreneur. That is why your faith must be the foundation for what you do in addition to proper planning as well as execution. One thing I see others do that lead to their own demise is instead of doing the work, they blame others for not having what they desire and become jealous and resentful toward others who do.

Declare this aloud, *"I no longer play small, but I show up BIG!!!"* That is the mindset it is going to take as an entrepreneur. Sure, you will have challenges but in the midst of reconditioning your mind you will learn how to develop opposition into opportunities! That was good huh? Alright enough small talk. Are you ready to dive into Part I?

I'm sure you have figured it out already that *yes,* I have included part I of my three part self-study coaching program right here absolutely free for you within the pages of this book! This is my way of saying thank you for believing enough in yourself to invest in you because I too am invested in you!

Within this exclusive program, *How to Fire Your Boss & Hire Yourself as COO* it is broken down into 3 parts:

- Your Role as COO

- Mind Transformation

- 2 Step Process to Exiting Your Job

Although the bread and butter is found in Mind Transformation and the 2 Step Process to Existing Your Job. You will have to enroll in my program to gain the details of that. But are you ready to learn why I focus on you being the COO rather than the CEO of your life (which is what many business coaches teach that I, as a Kingdom Entrepreneur do not agree with).

Before we dive in, I want to encourage you to:

The first step to transforming your life is to BELIEVE that you can and to know that you deserve BETTER! Good is okay, but why settle for when you can experience BETTER? Exactly!

You may say, my family or spouse doesn't support me. Who is going to be my customer? Who is going to help me further my vision? I can assure you that as you "Step Out to Find Out" and remain (1) dedicated, (2) consistent (3) operate in excellence; and let me add one here, refuse to divorce your vision, people will come from the north, south, east, and west to support your vision.

Usually when you step out and begin to pursue your dreams it's not the people you have known all your life that jump on board. Usually, it's those whom you may have met on social media, or in the line at Wal-Mart. It's not always those who share your last name that will stand with you and help build your vision.

Before we dive in, I want you to write out in the table below what you desired to learn where you hear the phrase: Fire Your BO$$ and notate it in the box below. When you purchase this program, you also receive a 30 minute one on one coaching session with me. You can learn where you can access this program at the end of this chapter.

What Specific Questions Do You Have in Regard to Transitioning into Full Time Entrepreneurship?

Module I: Your Role as COO & Proper Goal Setting

I'm sure you noticed that the title of this program was not entitled, *"Fire Your Boss & Hire Yourself as CEO,"* but it said, *"Fire Your Boss & Hire Yourself as COO!"* Upon investing in this program did you think, *'COO? Wouldn't I be the CEO?'* I intentionally said COO (Chief Operating Officer) which basically means, second in command.

If you are leaving your job to operate full time as an entrepreneur, then who is the CEO? Now, being a spiritual person (let's be clear I am spiritual NOT spooky) and for me Jesus Christ is the head of my life. Now I am not here to play the religion game with you for that is not currently my focus. But I am here to say, that regardless, who you choose to believe in you must be honest and admit there is a much higher being that was able to form this world, cause your mother to give birth to you as well as create this beautiful place we call Earth in which we all live in today.

Absolutely! So, now that you see that I am not trying to push my faith on you and we agree that there is a higher being who is much smarter, who is omnipresent and omnipotent in which we are not. Would this be correct?

With that being the case, the perspective I am teaching from within this program is living life as an entrepreneur in the role of COO rather than CEO (Chief Executive Officer). Too often we take the credit for what only God (or a higher being) can do. Would you agree? Now I am not here to debate but what I am saying is, come on you didn't create yourself therefore, you are incapable of functioning by yourself. We all have a leader. Some choose to believe their leader is a physical being or one who has passed on, while I choose to believe in the power of a true and living Savior, named Jesus Christ who is the Chief Orchestrator of my life.

Now again this may not be your belief but in whoever or whatever you believe in that person must be the **CEO (Chief Executive Officer)** and you must be willing to be to COO (Chief Operating Officer).

Simply put a **COO** is also known as the President or one who is "Second in Command." The responsibilities of the **COO** are to handle the daily operations of the company and report directly to the **CEO.**

Now, the **CEO** on the other hand is also known as what I call, the **HPIC** (Head Person in Charge) who is the one who provides clarity and direction of the vision, and you are then directed to carry it out.

Do you see how these correlate to our ultimate creation as human beings? We were each birthed with purpose and for purpose. Therefore, we receive our direction and purpose from our Creator then we simply execute the vision He gives us!

Once you have identified what your purpose and vision is for your life you are then able to walk it out daily by establishing what I call **S.M.A.R.T.** Goals to help you accomplish everything you set out to do.

As it relates to developing S.M.A.R.T. Goals as I previously mentioned here is a breakdown for this proven system that is guaranteed to work if you work it!

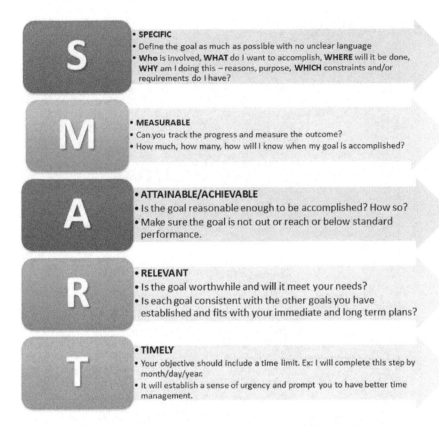

- **SPECIFIC**
  - Define the goal as much as possible with no unclear language
  - **Who** is involved, **WHAT** do I want to accomplish, **WHERE** will it be done, **WHY** am I doing this – reasons, purpose, **WHICH** constraints and/or requirements do I have?

- **MEASURABLE**
  - Can you track the progress and measure the outcome?
  - How much, how many, how will I know when my goal is accomplished?

- **ATTAINABLE/ACHIEVABLE**
  - Is the goal reasonable enough to be accomplished? How so?
  - Make sure the goal is not out or reach or below standard performance.

- **RELEVANT**
  - Is the goal worthwhile and will it meet your needs?
  - Is each goal consistent with the other goals you have established and fits with your immediate and long term plans?

- **TIMELY**
  - Your objective should include a time limit. Ex: I will complete this step by month/day/year.
  - It will establish a sense of urgency and prompt you to have better time management.

Before I could live my dream of becoming a full time entrepreneur, I used this above system and took my commitments very seriously because I knew the ratio or statistics for the average entrepreneur to survive after five years was less likely.

I remember reading this status quo and telling myself, *"This doesn't apply to me because I am not average!"* The day you exchange being average or mediocre living is the day you begin to LIVE OUT LOUD!

That is also what it means to be the **COO** of your life-Acknowledging there is a higher being leading you and whose mission you are fulfilling in the Earth by your existence. Life is not all about you although you will be able to enjoy the fruit of your labor. But life is about helping, coaching, mentoring and leading others along the way. It is time to stop allowing life to happen to you and you must begin happening to life! The first way to do that is to make a decision to STEP OUT OF THE BOX!

You may be the first entrepreneur, innovator or even millionaire in your family and you must be okay with that. Instead of viewing it as a challenge view yourself as a trailblazer who is blazing a trail for others in your family to follow; showing them the only limits that exist are those we put on ourselves.

Considering we are here on goal setting I want to not only teach you practical skills to help you fire your boss and hire yourself as COO but I also want to show you how to apply this system to your overall life.

Practical Step #1-
SET GOALS Using the S.M.A.R.T. System listed above:

Practical Step #2-
Identify WHY Goal Setting is Important:

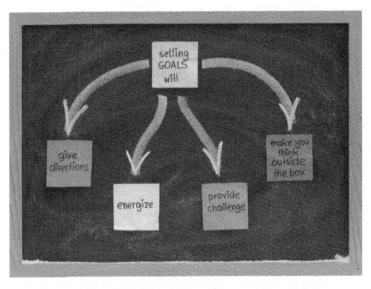

Practical Step #3:
Identify The Common Mistakes People Make in Goal Setting:

My advice to you is to begin to practice implementing the above system in your everyday life as a whole so when you are ready to transition off of your job these strategies you will already have in place, and which will in turn make your process more bearable and encouraging.

Truth is the entrepreneur life automatically comes with its own struggles, discomfort, and stresses, therefore, the more you do to prepare now the smoother (not easier) the transition will be for you. The top two things I teach when speaking to aspiring entrepreneurs is that the success of a full-time entrepreneur is contingent upon three things:

a) Mindset

b) Ability

c) Dedication

This is so true because even when you desire to upgrade your financial status from a hundred-aire, to a thousand-aire, to even a millionaire you will have to first transition in your MIND first. Before you ever accumulate the money physically you must prepare your mind to receive it mentally.

The next is ability. We each have a certain level of drive, momentum, and desire on the inside of us. But just like anything else those things must be fed in order to be strengthened. Just as iron sharpens iron, entrepreneurs fuel the strength and increase the wavelength of other entrepreneurs. This is why I am a firm believer of this quote by Darrin Henson, *"Whom you assemble you will soon resemble,"* We are who we surround ourselves with. Therefore it's important to monitor your inner circle and do what I call a "Circle Check" daily.

Lastly, there is dedication. Simply wanting to be successful in life is not enough to obtain it and experience. You must be dedicated, committed and willing to preserve against all odds. Successful entrepreneurs are not only dreamers but they

are doers. They walk the walk and not simply talk the talk. Sarah from Trinidad says, "In order to experience your best life you must get rid of the boat riders and surround yourself with water walkers!" This is one of the most powerful quotes I have grabbed a hold of and refuse to let go.

Why so? Life as an entrepreneur is no joke! I am going to be completely honest with you in this program. I am not going to paint a false hope for you, but I want you to know exactly what you are getting yourself in and also know that everything you desire to have is possible. Too often we look externally versus internally for the answers to the many problems we face. When you remember that you are the COO of your life, you understand that your CEO is the HPIC (Head Person in Charge) therefore, it is not your place to worry but when things get tough or when you need clarity or further validation that you are on the right track, you go back to the CEO and gain reassurance needed to press through another day.

Your CEO is the ultimate visionary, and it is His vision that is placed within you that you were created to birth and walk out every day of your life. This is why having dreams, goals and visions all tie in together.

Have you considered what the vision is for your life? What does success look like to you? As we move forward in this course it is important that you take a moment to identify what success looks like to...YOU! Your definition of success may not be someone else's definition of success.

Want to know my definition of success? Success to me is when one is fulfilling his/her ultimate purpose in the Earth; the reason they were created/born. That to me is success. Success or wealth is not all about money. If you are launching a business in an effort to get rich, I encourage you to rethink it. Because your passion and desire alone will make you a lot of money. But once you have accumulated all the money and have bought all of the tangible items you desire then what? Will it really satisfy? Operating in your divine purpose is the only thing that will satisfy.

With that being said, take a moment and answer the following questions below:

1. WHAT does success look like to YOU?

_____

_____

_____

_____

_____

2. WHY do YOU desire to be an entrepreneur?

_____

_____

_____

_____

_____

3. WHAT type of business do YOU desire to have?

_____

_____

_____

_____

_____

4. WHAT do you bring to the table that is different from your competitors?

_____

_____

_____

_____

_____

5. HOW soon are you looking to advance into full time
   entrepreneurship?

   _____

   _____

6. Do you BELIEVE it is possible for YOU?

   _____

   _____

7. Are you willing to DO THE WORK?

   _____

   _____

After you have answered the above questions, you are prepared
and ready to move forward into the actual program where I share a
6 step guide to transitioning into full time entrepreneurship! Visit
www.CarlaCannon.com to learn more about this program and how
you can enter the next phase to making your dream a reality!

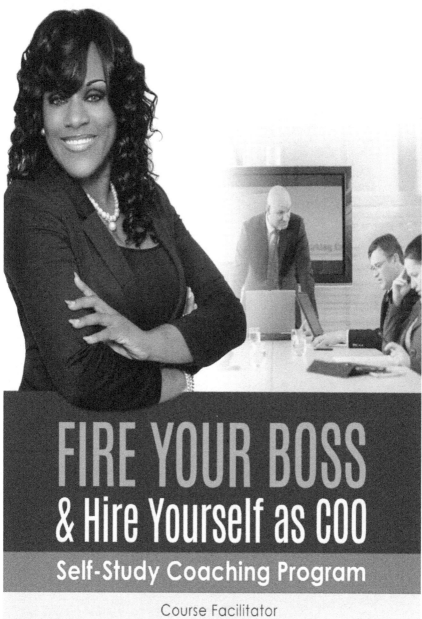

More Books & Products by Carla R. Cannon Available at
www.CarlaCannon.com:

WWW.CARLACANNON.COM

About the Author

Carla R. Cannon also known as "The Trailblazer" is indeed one of *God's Moguls* in the making. With her eloquent yet transparent approach she is committed to empowering global women from the pulpit to the marketplace on how to operate authentically and un-apologetically in their divine calling with a spirit of excellence.

Carla is a mother of a beautiful daughter, Patience, National Best Selling Author, Conference Host and Kingdom Entrepreneur who currently resides in North Carolina. One of the key areas Carla specializes in is teaching others how to profit from their pain by developing their storm into a story and their mess into a movement. Carla currently runs and operates Carla R. Cannon Enterprises, LLC which houses Cannon Publishing where she has served as the spiritual midwife of dozens of men and women on how to Write the Book Already and produce Revenue Rivers to provide for their families.

Carla is also the leader of a global movement, *Women of Standard*, where her mission is to make Jesus famous and in an effort in doing so she has hosted her very own tours: Women of Standard Experience and The Entrepreneur Blueprint where her mission was to activate Kingdom Entrepreneurs using the strategies within the pages of this book.

The testimony of this young woman of faith and her ability to share her story unashamed and with such boldness and conviction is truly what causes her to connect with others on multiple levels. Whether she is speaking to an audience of 1 or 1,000 the energy Carla exudes is magnetic, and contagious for she always leaves her audience not only feeling hopeful but with the tools to pursue their dreams and move further into their path of purpose. She is truly a woman after God's own heart and lives her life not trying to correct all of her wrongs but to learn and grow from them daily.

C   arla has been privileged to be featured on multiple radio talk shows including The Jewel Tankard Show (featuring Jewel Tankard from the hit show, *Thicker Than Water*.) Carla has also shared platforms with many prominent leaders such as Dr. Yvonne Capehart, Real Talk Kim, Jekalyn Carr, Tera C. Hodges, Dr. Jamal Bryant to name a few!

In 2014 Carla was invited to cover media for Bishop T. D. Jakes' annual Woman Thou Art Loosed Conference where tens of thousands of women and men assembled together. Carla's message is simple: *If God can use me, surely He can use YOU!*

Connect with Carla today on social media at: CarlaRCannon! Also, subscribe to her you tube channel to be inspired and equipped daily!

To contact Carla directly email her at:
Carla@womenofstandard.org

Mailing Address:
P.O. Box 29176
Charlotte, NC 28229

Books I Recommend on Business:

Secrets of Closing the Sale- Zig Ziglar

The Success Principles- Jack Canfield

Secrets of the Millionaire Mind- T. Harv Eker

Start Your Own Business-Staff of Entrepreneur Media

Think & Grow Rich- Dale Carnegie

Purple Cow- Seth Godin

Who Moved My Cheese-Dr. Spencer Johnson

The Power Playbook – La La Anthony

How to Win Friends and Influence People- Dale Carnegie

How Successful People Think- John Maxwell

Million Dollar Women- Julia Pimsleur

MONEY: Master the Game- Tony Robbins

The Money Makeover-Dave Ramsey

Book Me to Speak

To book Carla to come and speak at your event email us at Admin@womenofstandard.org using the word: "Booking" in the subject line. Carla specializes in speaking at conferences, workshops, seminars, and retreats both large and intimate settings!

Made in United States
North Haven, CT
14 July 2023

39056805R00114